While I Breathe

SUSAN M. REYNOLDS

GLASSSPIDERPUBLISHING

To my children Ryan, Christian, and Julia
- you inspire me every day.

"For everything there is a season,
a time for every activity under heaven..."
-Ecclesiastes 3:1 NLT

Chapter One

It was a day no mother should ever experience. My two-year-old son lay close to death as I waited to give birth to his baby brother via C-section.

"Don't worry," Ryan's nurse said. "We've got him."

But there had never been a single minute in the past two years that I hadn't worried.

God bless my little boy. He had tried his hardest, but after two years of bedside vigils and prayers, he had little fight left. I wanted to hold him forever but was hardly ever allowed to hold him at all. And there was nothing I could do to make him better.

The sorrow I felt as I gazed down at Ryan's swollen face was unbearable. My firstborn son was suffering from lung and heart disease—his tiny lungs so scarred and damaged that they resembled white clouds in X-rays; his precious heart had worked so hard to compensate that it had led to irreparable damage. By this point, he was fully dependent on life support, unable to eat or breathe on his own. The drugs the doctors had given him to manage his pain and anxiety had made him physically addicted. Imagine, a two-year-old addicted to Ativan and Fentanyl.

I closed my eyes and prayed. "God, I don't know your plan, but please, *please* watch over Ryan and ease his suffering." I leaned over and kissed his forehead. "I love you, little lamb," I whispered.

His eyes were slits of exhaustion and sadness. He looked at me as if to ask, "Is this goodbye?"

"How am I supposed to do this?" Tears streamed down my face.

The nurse wrapped her arms around me. "He *knows* you love him. He *feels* it. Go bring his baby brother into the world and celebrate this new life. I promise you, we will be right here with Ryan."

I put my hand on Ryan's chest and felt it rise and fall in sync with the ventilator. My God, how this little boy inspired me! His will to live against all odds over these past two years had been astonishing. Like a boxer in a ring getting knocked down over and over again, he kept standing back up in defiance. His strength gave *me* strength and had always given me hope. Gratitude for the privilege of being his mom now outweighed my fading hope.

"RyRy, I have to leave now, but I'll be back tomorrow." I felt physical pain in my heart, like it was splintering to pieces.

Walking away from Ryan that morning felt like a betrayal. I had been by his side for over two years. Loving him. Praying for him. Advocating for him. Reading to him. Cheering him on when he was well enough to do physical therapy. Massaging his broken little body in his hospital bed whenever he was back on life support.

He was my purpose. Every morning, I woke up, put my armor on, and went to battle to protect and save this beautiful child. Now what was I to do? I felt guilty for the excitement I felt in knowing I would soon meet my new son, and a deep, aching sadness for the suffering Ryan was continuing to endure. I was helpless to heal him, and that knowledge was shredding me.

John, my husband, led me out of Ryan's room and out of the intensive care unit. After a brief walk down a few hallways, we reached the maternity ward. This would be my second C-section. I was afraid, but not nearly as afraid as I had been the first time.

At least I'd known this C-section was coming. And knowing more about what to expect makes a big difference. I was desperate for the outcome to be different this time. But would it? It would if prayers worked...but do prayers work? They hadn't for Ryan.

When Dr. Hanson entered the room, I searched his eyes for affirmation that all would be okay. He didn't even have to say a word. Looking into his eyes, I knew he'd not let anything happen to my baby.

"You ready?" he asked.

I nodded and put my body and my baby in his care.

As they positioned me on the table, my mind drifted back two years, to the day Ryan was born.

It was a sunny day in late August. I was thirty-two weeks pregnant and looking forward to relaxing for the final two months before my baby came.

"Good morning!" I smiled as my friend Megan and her two-year-old, Jack, got into my car for a trip to the city where Jack was going to audition at a modeling agency. Seeing Jack with his bright-blue eyes and chubby, dimpled cheeks filled me with excitement that soon I'd have my own baby.

As I sat thumbing through magazines in the waiting room during the audition, I thought, "I'm going to do this with my child, too. Then Megan and I can do this together!"

Thinking of that moment still brings me a smile, even though it was to be the last "normal" moment of my life.

After returning from the city, we lunched on Megan's deck, chatting away and soaking up the warm afternoon sun, but something felt off.

"Hey, Meg." I shielded my eyes and looked at her. "I haven't felt the baby move all morning. Do you think something could be wrong?"

"It's probably just because we were busy in New York," she said. "And this is the first time you've been able to relax."

"Yeah, you're probably right."

"I'm sure everything is fine," she said reassuringly. "Try not to worry."

I wanted to believe her, but I *was* worried, so I headed home. When I got there, our yellow lab, Jake, bounded over to me. His tail wagged like an out-of-control windshield wiper as I patted his head.

"Hungry, sweet boy?" I asked, kneeling to him. He licked my face and I laughed. I grabbed a snack for each of us and sat with Jake, his head on my lap.

I became increasingly aware of the stillness in my belly. Another hour passed. I still wasn't feeling the baby move. I drank a glass of milk. Nothing. Then a glass of juice. Nothing. Finally, I called the doctor. They told me to come right in.

It was now 7 p.m. I was in the waiting room for thirty excruciating minutes before I was called into an examination room.

"Let's see what's happening," the nurse said as she positioned me on the chair and wrapped a belt around my abdomen, hooking me up to a monitor to perform a "non-stress test."

"What does this do?" I asked.

"It will give us information about the baby's heart rate and movements," she told me. "We'll monitor it for about twenty to thirty minutes, so just sit back and relax."

Ten minutes went by.

"Do you feel anything?" she asked.

"No, nothing." I was lying perfectly still, desperate to feel even the slightest kick.

Fifteen minutes later, the nurse left the room. I tried to calm myself by taking deep breaths but felt as if I couldn't get enough air. Worry was overtaking me, both emotionally and physically. My shoulders tensed and I clenched my fists.

Finally, the doctor entered. "It's good that you called and came in," he told me. "I'm concerned about irregularities with your baby's heart rate. I want you to go over to the hospital for an ultrasound."

"Now?"

"Yes, right now. I'll call to tell them to be ready for you. You should call your husband and let him know. Do you have a cell phone?"

I shook my head.

"Use the office phone." He pointed to the wall.

I called John and left frantic messages on his office phone and at home. "Something is wrong with the baby and they're sending me to the hospital. Where are you? Please come when you get this message."

I checked the time. It was 9 p.m.

"I can't reach him," I told the doctor. "I'll try again when I get to the hospital." I reached for my purse and pulled out my car keys.

The doctor stopped me. "I can't let you drive," he said. "You'll need a ride."

"Why can't I drive?" I asked him.

"Your baby may be in distress, so it's best if you don't."

"Well, what am I supposed to do?" I asked.

"I'll drive her, doctor," the nurse said.

I tightened my arms around my belly. "What about my car? How will I get it later?"

"Don't worry about that," the nurse said. "Your husband can figure it out."

Feeling more frightened with each breath, I followed the nurse to her car. Sitting in the passenger seat, my body tensed and my breathing accelerated. She reached across to me. "Focus on taking deep, slow breaths."

As we pulled into the hospital parking lot, I remembered how excited I used to feel at the prospect of arriving there one day to have my baby. Now an ominous feeling washed over me as we approached.

I was rushed into the ultrasound room where a resident began the test, moving a wand around my belly. After a few minutes, she asked, "Have you been taking drugs during your pregnancy?"

"I was on an antibiotic at the end of the first trimester for an infection," I said, "but nothing else since. Why?"

And then it struck me. She had meant *actual* drugs. At that moment, I knew something must have been very wrong. But how could it? I ate right. I didn't smoke. I didn't drink. I'd altered my workout routine to ensure the safety of the baby. I practiced breathing exercises to control my stress. I took my prenatal vitamins daily and followed the *What to Expect When You're Expecting* book like a bible. I had done everything that I was supposed to do. How in God's name could my baby be at risk?

"What is wrong with my baby?" I pleaded.

"It looks too small for thirty-two weeks," she said. "I'll go get Dr. Jackson, and he can answer your questions."

Dr. Jackson entered the ultrasound room, took one look at the picture and measurements on the screen, and said, "You need an emergency C-section."

"Oh, my God, no," I whispered.

My whole world began to fall apart. I had thought I was going to be one of the lucky ones: a young mother with a beautiful, healthy baby, an adoring husband, a great house. I had never been so blessed in my life. But that dream was about to change in a way I could never have imagined—and I suppose that was a good thing. Because if someone had told me the decisions, struggles, sadness, and suffering that lay ahead, I couldn't possibly have hung onto the hope that kept me going.

It was now 10 p.m. Within minutes, various hospital personnel arrived and the bombardment began. Someone helped me to replace my clothes with a hospital gown. Another poked and prodded, trying to find a vein for the IV. Another placed sticky patches on various parts of my body to monitor my vital signs.

"We need your signature on this form," someone said as they slid a clipboard in front of me.

Throughout all of this, I used the hospital phone beside me, dialing in desperation, trying to reach John for probably the tenth time. I tried every family member and every friend. Nobody was answering their damn phones. How could *no one* be home?

I left messages everywhere. "Hi, I'm at the hospital. Something's wrong with the baby and I'm having an emergency C-section in a few minutes! I'm alone and can't reach John…"

"I'm so sorry," someone said as they took the handset from me. "We have to go."

"Dr. Jackson, can't we wait just a bit until someone can be with her?" a nurse asked.

"No," he told her. "We have to go *now.*"

I was wheeled into the operating room as tears streamed down my face and my body trembled. Delivering the baby early was bad enough. Having to go through it alone was terrifying.

The anesthesiologist gave me an epidural so I would feel nothing from the waist down. The nurse inserted a urinary catheter.

I stared up at the ceiling, feeling as if my body were no longer my own. Tears soaked the sides of my face and left wet circles on the pillow under my head.

"Is she alone?" I heard one of the surgical nurses ask.

It happened quickly. Within minutes of Dr. Jackson asking for the scalpel, my baby was out.

"It's a boy," someone said.

And then silence.

"Why isn't he crying?" I asked. "Is he okay?"

No one answered.

There was a sudden rush of activity as my baby was carried to a table on the other side of the room where a team of people in blue scrubs surrounded him. Their hands and bodies moved in unison as they tried to save my baby's life. Sounds I couldn't identify and words I didn't understand filled the room: *Cyanotic. IUGR. Suction. Intubate. Ventilator.*

"How's he doing?" Dr. Jackson asked with urgency in his voice.

"Two pounds nine ounces," someone called out.

"Why is he so small?" I asked, demanding an answer. "Shouldn't he be bigger?"

Again, there was no answer.

"Apgar 4. Intubating now."

The room was spinning. I held onto every word and every thread of emotional strength I could muster. Dr. Jackson sewed me up as the medical team attempted to stabilize my baby. I felt like I was treading water in the middle of the ocean with no rescue boat in sight.

The nurse leaned over me and smiled. "Your husband is here."

I stared at her blankly. Having just endured the trauma alone, I could only wonder where he'd been and why I hadn't been able to reach him. The door opened, and John rushed in wearing hospital scrubs, paper booties over his shoes, and a nervous smile.

He grabbed my hand and kissed my forehead. My body softened under his touch, but my eyes couldn't hide my confusion and distress.

Within moments, the team rushed our baby out, allowing us only a moment to see him. I saw a flash of optimism in John's eyes. Maybe he saw a newborn baby; the start of a beautiful life. I saw a very tiny, very sick baby who'd just been cut out of my stomach, with a tube coming out of his mouth and a multitude of wires covering his body.

"Where are you taking him?" I begged.

"They need to get him to the Neonatal Intensive Care Unit to get him stabilized," Dr. Jackson said.

I felt utterly useless. My baby needed me in the desperately, yet there was nothing at that moment that I would be allowed to do for him.

I turned to John. "I couldn't reach you. I was so scared. Where were you?"

"I'm so sorry," he said. "I got here as fast as I could."

The momentary comfort I felt as he stood beside me was slowly overtaken by sorrow and anger. I couldn't deal with that just yet. "John, please go follow the baby and make sure he's okay."

"I want to stay here and make sure *you're* okay."

"I need you to find out what is happening. Please go find him. *Please.*"

"One of the staff at the nurses' station will guide you to him," Dr. Jackson offered. "Your wife will be in recovery for a while."

Still, John hesitated. "Go!" I ordered. "Please!"

I had needed him to be with me and hold my hand when my world collapsed. Now that it was over, I needed him to go find our baby to make sure he was still alive.

The doctor motioned with his head for John to go.

"Okay, I'll be right back," John said. He squeezed my hand and left.

It was now eerily quiet as Dr. Jackson finished the last of the stitches.

"Is my baby going to be okay?"

"It's good you came in when you did," he said. "A few more

hours, and he would have died. For now, he's in one of the best neonatal units in the state."

"But is he going to be *okay?*"

"He's very sick. His lungs are underdeveloped, so he's not able to breathe on his own. At this point, all we can do is wait."

"Why did this happen?" I wept. "And why is he so small? He should be at least four pounds at thirty-two weeks, shouldn't he?"

"It seems he must have stopped growing at some point, and we don't yet know why. I'll come to check on you tomorrow, and we can talk more then."

I closed my eyes, feeling helpless, hoping and praying that when the sun rose, my baby would still be alive.

After a short time, John returned. "The team is working on getting him stabilized."

He's still alive. Thank God, I thought.

When I was in recovery, John told me that his brother Brad had been the one to let him know what was happening and that Brad suggested John stop at home first to pack a bag for me.

"That's why I was delayed getting here," he said and showed me the duffle bag.

"You went home first?" My sadness and frustration turned to fury. I looked away. I often didn't feel like I was a priority. But this. *This* was at a whole new level.

I was moved to a hospital room after 1 a.m. As the nurse wheeled my bed out of the recovery room, I begged, "Can I please see my baby before I go to my room? *Please?*"

I saw her eyes. She was about to say no, but there was no way she could deny me. She wheeled me down several hallways and turned the final corner into the neonatal unit. My brain was still foggy from the effects of the anesthesia, and my body felt numb. I struggled to take in all that was before me. My bed came to a stop next to where my baby was lying.

I stared at him, absorbing what I could amid my exhaustion. There was no sign of life in him. Only the sounds of the machines that kept him alive. I saw the looks of concern and sympathy on the faces of the NICU nurses.

"Oh, my God," I gasped.

At that moment, the sounds and voices surrounding me felt like echoes in my head. I closed my eyes, asking God for a miracle.

I wanted to stay there with him, my bed right next to his, but the nurse said, "Let's get you to your room."

Just six hours had passed since I'd arrived at Dr. Jackson's office, yet it felt as if an entire day had gone by. Arriving at my room, I saw a woman asleep in the bed closest to the door. I was surprised to have a roommate but was too dazed to care.

John was beside me, emptying the duffle bag of a flannel Christmas nightgown, a sweatshirt, a denim jacket, a toothbrush, a curling iron, and hair spray. "Here, you may need these tonight."

I looked at him, baffled. "What were you thinking? It's the end of August."

"You get cold easily, so I wanted you to have things to keep you warm."

He was right. I did get cold easily. But I didn't need the things in the bag, and I certainly wasn't going to wake up and curl my hair.

As much as I appreciated that he thought he was helping, I couldn't look at him, and I didn't want comfort from him. I didn't want to hear that everything was going to be okay. To this day, I can't remember what his reason was for not answering my calls, or where he said he'd been. Maybe I blocked it out. Maybe it got lost in the midst of all of the chaos. At that point, it didn't matter.

It was now 2 a.m.

"I'm going to head home now," John said. "Get some sleep." He kissed the top of my head and left.

I lay quietly, trying to stifle my tears so my roommate wouldn't hear me. But the weight of all that had happened was hitting me, and all I wanted to do was sob myself to sleep.

"Hi, I'm Liz," came a voice from the other bed.

I grabbed a tissue and wiped my face. "I'm Susan. Sorry to wake you."

"Are you okay?"

"Yes, but I don't know about my baby. I just had emergency surgery, and he almost died."

"Oh, I'm so sorry," Liz said. Her compassion was comforting.

"Thank you. How is your baby?"

"She's fine. She's resting in the nursery."

"Congratulations." I didn't know what else to say.

The night was torture. I fell asleep eventually but was soon jolted awake by Liz's newborn crying. My throat tightened and my breaths became shallow. I couldn't stop my tears.

I remembered I could call the NICU to check on my baby. My mind was scrambled with questions when I was put on hold. What if he'd died but they waited until morning to tell me? That would mean I'd never get the chance to see him or hold him. Or what if he was still alive but near death? I would have to get to him quickly! But how was I going to do that? Did they allow visitors this early? I was racked with anguish. I knew the only thing that would help would be to lay my eyes on him, but I needed someone to help me get there.

When a NICU nurse answered, I said, "Hello, I had a baby last night, and I'm calling to see how he is."

She asked me my name, and I told her. Then she put me on hold. Less than a minute later, someone picked up. "Hello, Mrs. Wilson, I've been your son's night nurse."

I asked how he was doing. She told me he was critical but stable.

"So he is still alive?" I asked, and she told me yes. I thanked her and rested my hand on my heart. There was still time to get to him and hold him, I thought. Was he wondering where I was and why I wasn't with him? Did he feel alone and scared like me? I was desperate to see him and to let him know I was there.

"Good morning. How are you feeling?" My thoughts were interrupted by the floor nurse coming in to check my vital signs. "It's time for more pain meds if you need them," she said.

"Yes," I said. "Please." My lower abdomen felt like it had knives moving around inside of it.

The nurse handed me a cup of pills and a glass of water. "We have lactation consultants here that speak to all new moms," she told me. "Are you planning to breastfeed your baby?"

Clearly, she didn't know my situation. "He's in the NICU, so I'm not sure I can."

Her expression softened. "Okay, well, you can pump your milk and freeze it for now until we know what's going on."

I didn't even know what that meant, but I nodded.

"I'll have someone come in to speak with you," she said and

smiled. "In the meantime, are you ready to try to walk just a bit? It's time to remove your catheter, and then I can help you to the bathroom to wash up if you'd like."

My desire to get moving was the most primal force I'd ever experienced. I needed to get to my baby. With sheer will, I slid myself off the side of the bed. The nurse wrapped her arm around my waist as I stood.

"Okay," I exhaled. "I'm ready."

With my face washed and my teeth brushed, I fell back into bed. Those simple acts took every bit of strength I had. I fell back to sleep until John arrived about an hour later. Shortly thereafter, two doctors came in.

"Mr. and Mrs. Wilson, I'm Dr. Kanton, your baby's neonatologist. This is Dr. Thomas, your son's cardiologist."

"Cardiologist?" I asked, puzzled. "Is our baby okay?"

"He's very small and very sick," Dr. Kanton began to explain.

"But he will get better, right? *Right?*"

"At this point, it's hour by hour," she said. "We're doing everything we can for him, but you need to know that he's on life support and is in critical condition."

I felt sick and swallowed the bile that rose in my throat.

Dr. Thomas stepped forward. "I'm here because your baby has a heart defect in one of the upper chambers of his heart. It's called an atrial septal defect, ASD for short, and may be caused by a syndrome, but we're not yet sure. We're going to watch it for now, but it may be an indicator of a larger problem."

"I don't understand," I said. "What possible larger problem? Why do you think he has a syndrome?"

Dr. Kanton took over. "Your son has a few physical characteristics, including the ASD, that may indicate a syndrome," she said. "Because he's so tiny, his features aren't developed enough to draw any type of concrete conclusion, so we can't confirm anything without genetic testing. We've drawn some blood and should have results in about a week."

"What syndrome? What *could* it be? Is it Down syndrome?"

"It would be inappropriate to make any guesses at this point," she replied.

"But if you think this, then you must have *some* idea of what it is!" I could feel my face flushing. John took my hand.

"We need to wait for the results of the test. For now, get some rest, and we'll keep you updated."

They left, and John and I looked at each other, stunned. I had to get to my baby, to hold him and let him know that everything would be okay. He had to know that I would protect him.

"Let's go see him," I said. "Can you find me a wheelchair please?"

"Yes, I will," John said, "but before we go, I think we should discuss having him baptized."

"Well, of course we'll have him baptized."

"No, I mean now. Like today. Just in case. I was speaking to the hospital chaplain, and he can arrange to do it as soon as we're ready."

My voice cracked when I asked, "You mean in case he dies?"

"Yes. I'm sorry, but we want to be sure his soul is protected, right?"

It hadn't occurred to me that this tiny, innocent baby would receive anything other than the open arms of Heaven should he be taken.

"Then we need to give him a name," I said. "He can't be

baptized as 'baby boy Wilson.'" I straightened my shoulders and lifted my chin.

We made a quick list of our favorite names and chose those with meanings that spoke to us. After passing on several, I asked, "What does Ryan mean?"

John flipped through the pages of the baby name book. "Ryan means 'little king.'"

I closed my eyes and nodded. "That's it. That's his name." I smiled knowing that our tiny baby would be our little king.

We moved on to the middle name and chose Christopher, after the saint, because Ryan desperately needed his help to live. Then we called the NICU, proudly sharing our son's new name with his nurse. 'Baby boy Wilson' became Ryan Christopher.

I squeezed John's hand. "Can you please go find me that wheelchair now?"

The Neonatal Intensive Care Unit at this hospital was state of the art at that time, and it was enormous. There were babies in warmers and incubators. In my post-surgery, medically in-duced haze twelve hours earlier, I hadn't been able to observe my surroundings. Now, in the clear light of day, I was able to take it all in. I felt like I was visiting a foreign land on a tour with a group of strangers.

As we approached the area where our baby was, I felt a wave of nausea come over me. "John, I feel really sick. Oh, God. I feel like I'm going to throw up!!"

Before I knew it, I was vomiting, right into the water fountain near the scrubbing station. There were people nearby who saw, and I was mortified.

John handed me a paper towel. As I wiped my mouth, a nurse came to help.

"I'm so sorry," I said in utter embarrassment. "How do I clean this?"

"Don't worry about that, we'll take care of it," she said and put her hand on my shoulder. "When was your baby born?"

"Late last night. It was an emergency, and I only got to see him for a minute." I choked back a sob.

"Okay, let's get you to him." She led us to the sink and explained the strict procedures we'd have to follow every time before entering the NICU, including gowning up and doing a two-minute handwashing process.

Still feeling queasy, I sat in the wheelchair at the sink, counting to 120 as I scrubbed my hands and forearms.

The noise upon entering was piercing. Machines of all different shapes and sizes landscaped the room, and from them came loud pulsing beeps and earsplitting alarms, like sirens. People were everywhere—tiny babies with parents at their bedsides, nurses, and multiple medical staff tending to each baby.

I felt eyes on me as my wheelchair was pushed to the edge of the open contraption holding my baby's tiny, translucent body. His fragility seized my heart. Never had I felt such love.

I searched his face for some kind of resemblance to me or John, but half of his face was covered by tape that held a tube in place. Other tubes and wires covered every part of his body. I stared at him, seeing for the first time all of the blood vessels and the discoloration of his skin. Except for his diaper, he was naked.

"Oh, my God, John," I whispered. "He's so small! He must be cold! Why isn't he covered?"

"I know this looks scary. Let me explain what's happening," his nurse said.

So began the crash course in taking care of neonates, learning about the mechanical ventilator that was breathing for him, the IV that was giving him nutrients, the wires all over his body monitoring his heart, and various other functions. Although I was scared and overwhelmed, all I could think about was how he must be feeling.

"Is he in pain?" I asked. "Why isn't he in an incubator?"

"We keep him open like this because he's in critical condition," she told us.

I learned quickly what that meant—that they needed immediate access to him in case he crashed and needed to be resuscitated.

"But isn't he cold?" I asked.

"No, because this bed is a 'warmer' and this light over him keeps his temperature regulated."

I still didn't understand any of it, but I trusted what she told me. I didn't know then, but I would soon begin to understand all of it acutely.

"May I hold him now?" I asked.

"Not yet. He's still very fragile."

That was not the answer I had been expecting. I had envisioned them wrapping him in a blanket and putting him in my arms as soon as I was able to get there. That was what I had been waiting for since they'd cut him out of me.

"Please?" I begged, my lower lip quivering. "I promise I'll be really careful. He needs to know I'm here. *I need him to know that I'm here! Please!*"

"I'm so sorry," the nurse said. "I wish you could. It's not safe yet, especially with all of the tubes and wires attached to him."

I looked at John in anguish.

"When might we be able to hold him?" he asked.

"Maybe in a few days. It's hard to say. But you can touch him and talk to him. I know that's not the same, but it will help him."

I sat next to Ryan's warmer with my hand resting on his body, hoping he could feel me, looking and listening to all of the foreign sounds, watching the machine breathing for him, his chest rising up and down, his little arms and legs twitching from time to time, resisting the need to pick him up and put him to my chest.

An hour passed with me just watching him. I was so absorbed in it that I didn't hear John when he suggested taking me back to my room. I wanted to stay but couldn't ignore my exhaustion and the pain that was once again creeping in. All I wanted to do was lie my head down next to my baby and sleep holding his tiny little hand.

I braced myself on the arms of the wheelchair and stood, placing my hand on his head. "I'll be back, sweet baby boy. You're not alone. I promise."

Chapter Two

I hated that I was jealous of my roommate for breastfeeding her newborn. This was my third roommate in three days, and I had minimal tolerance left. I stared and then began to cry. I just couldn't look any longer. Oh, how lucky she was.

I sat on the edge of the bed, hands folded in my lap, legs dangling from my maternity dress, and flip-flops on my feet, waiting to leave the hospital.

"Do you want to take these home?" my sister Paula asked as she gathered the flowers and balloons in my hospital room. The only thing I wanted to take home was my baby.

I started to say no to the flowers when John said, "Yes, let's bring them home. I'm going to go bring the car around. I'll meet you at the front door."

"I don't want the flowers. Or the balloons," I said to Paula after John had left.

"I know, but John wants to bring them home."

"What about what I want? I'm the one who gave birth—alone, by the way, with no help from him. Shouldn't my feelings matter?" My voice cracked.

Paula sat next to me and squeezed my hand. I was lost. "I don't know how to do this. How can I just leave him here?"

I was being discharged, forced to go home, leaving my critically ill three-day-old baby in the hands of strangers in a cold, shrill, chaotic environment. My close physical proximity to Ryan over the last few days had been my lifeline. Knowing he was within reach at any given moment allowed me to feel like a mom. What purpose would I have at home? Ryan was teetering on the edge of death. I would be thirty minutes away. Would I be able to get to him in time if something happened?

Torment filled me as I said goodbye to him earlier that morning.

"Ryan, I have to leave you, but I'll be back." Hot tears ran down my face. "I love you so much. Please stay strong and keep fighting. Please, Ryan."

I would have sold my soul to make time stop, to remain by my son's side, touching his tiny body, praying for him, loving him.

The squeaking of wheels outside of my room drew our attention as the wheelchair arrived. "Ready, Mrs. Wilson?"

Paula gave my hand a final squeeze. I sighed, straightened my shoulders, and pushed up off the bed.

My body was rigid as the nurse wheeled me down the hallway. Paula followed with the cart of gifts and flowers. Passersby smiled when they saw the balloons emblazoned with the words *Congratulations on your baby boy*, but the smiles gave way to looks of pity when they saw no baby in my arms.

Stay strong, I repeated in my head.

I held my breath as we entered the elevator, fully aware of the distance growing between me and my baby. It was a beautiful day outside, but I would have preferred to remain in that cold, dark hospital with my son, protecting him, loving him, reassuring him. My hands gripped the arms of my wheelchair as we approached the front door. I felt my throat close as I choked back a sob.

The massive doors opened to the sight of John smiling and holding a video camera aimed at my face. "Smile!" came his upbeat voice. "Congratulations, new mommy!"

I stifled the scream inside and forced a smile.

Paula was my rock. She fielded calls from friends asking if they should send baby gifts. I understood their hesitation. After all, each morning we woke up not knowing if Ryan would survive. Nobody wanted their gift to become a reminder of death. Besides, many wondered, do you send a gift for a critically ill baby? The answer is yes.

"That's sweet of them to ask," I told Paula. "All we need now are positive thoughts and prayers."

"I never got to throw you a baby shower," Paula lamented. "Maybe we can do a delayed shower? You'll need everything."

I hoped that day would one day come. "That sounds wonderful," I said.

I'd been in survival mode all week. Conversations with friends and family led to so many expressions of "I'm so sorry," magnifying the celebration that eluded us.

These reactions were an added part of the difficult course John and I faced. I didn't know how to manage my own emotional turmoil, much less help other people navigate their sadness.

I appreciated that their sorrow came from a place of love for me and my son. Most everyone had babies, and all were excited for us to be a part of the blissful experience of childbirth and parenting.

I visited Ryan each morning, grateful for every day that he survived. Every evening, I went back to say good night, hoping he could hear my voice and would know that I was there. It wasn't logical considering the fact that day and night don't exist for sick preemies in the NICU, but it was all I could do.

We were still awaiting the results of the genetic testing, and the first thought that crossed my mind every day when I awoke was, "Will this be the day?"

By the ninth day, my worries had come to own me. My face was drawn, and the circles underneath my eyes were darker than they had ever been. I remember sitting in my kitchen watching John in the backyard, strangely pacing back and forth with a phone to his ear.

Who's he talking to? I wondered as he disappeared from my view. I sipped my tea, struggling against the overwhelming stress. Jake lay asleep on the floor next to me. His head jerked up when the back door squeaked open. I put the teacup down, straightened my shoulders, and sat back with my hands clenched together in my lap.

John strode in, his lips tight, one hand rubbing the back of his neck. He didn't look at me but instead focused his gaze out the window as he collapsed into the chair beside me.

"Ryan has Down syndrome," he told me. "The doctor wants us to meet at the hospital."

His words hit me like a truck and I screamed. *"No!"* I pounded my hands on the butcher block table, the teacup wobbling, tea splattering everywhere. I stood up so forcefully that I sent the rickety chair to the floor.

"You were just talking to the doctor? Why didn't you tell me?" I screamed. "You just walk in and say that? With no warning?"

John simply sat there with his shoulders slumped in defeat and his face in his hands. "There was no easy way to tell you."

He was right. But I was still furious. Down syndrome? How could that be? The doctor was supposed to have been wrong!

"No!" I screamed again. "No!"

I tore around the room while Jake cowered in the corner. He wasn't used to emotional outbursts. I remember thinking I should have comforted him, but I had to escape.

"Oh, my God, this can't be!" I yelled, storming outside.

I was racked with physical and emotional pain. I fell to my knees on the grass as gut-wrenching sobs convulsed my entire body. My hope now shattered, I cried for myself, for my son, for my family, and for the loss of my dream of a perfect, healthy child.

I heard the back door open and saw Jake padding toward me. His caramel-colored eyes searched my face as if to ask, "Are you okay?" I reached out to him, and he rested his head in my lap, unfazed by my tears saturating his fur.

Jake's unconditional love was a gift. His gentleness calmed me and helped me breathe. His love was just what I needed. *Dog spelled backwards is God,* I thought. Was this a sign from God that I wasn't alone?

I hugged Jake and took a deep breath. "I need to pull it together. We have to be strong because Ryan needs us."

I was about to learn that I was just as capable of giving the same unconditional love to my beautiful, special son.

"No more crying," I told myself. What would it say about me

as a mother if I kept crying? That I didn't love my baby? Or worse, that I didn't want him? I loved my baby. I wanted him. But my shock confused me. I was a first-time mom with a one-week-old critically ill premature baby. And now we were told he had Down syndrome. There was nothing that could have prepared me for that.

An intense need to be with Ryan took over. I had to tell him that I loved him, no matter what. I walked back inside with Jake.

"Let's go to the hospital," I said to John.

We pulled into the hospital parking lot and circled until we found a spot. The moment the car stopped, I pulled at the door handle.

John reached over. "Wait."

I looked at him, my lips trembling, my fingers still gripping the door handle.

"Whatever happens," he said, "it's going to be okay."

I appreciated his positivity, but I didn't feel it. "How can you know that? We don't even know what we're dealing with."

My head was in conflict with my heart. There were too many unknowns. I had never been good with unknowns because my imagination would take me to the most worrisome outcomes. Would Ryan survive? What would Down syndrome mean for him and us as a family? How mentally and physically challenged would he be? Could I handle it? Could *we* handle it? It was as if those questions were creating an emotional wall built on fear that was blocking me from embracing the love filling my heart

When we got to the hospital lobby, my eyes went straight to a woman in a wheelchair holding her newborn baby with her husband by her side. I stood frozen, dazed, and stared at them—husband and wife smiling, radiating joy.

Jealousy engulfed me. That was supposed to be us.

John put his hand around my waist, guiding me to the elevator. He pushed the UP button. No doors opened. I looked at my watch. Over an hour had passed since the doctor had called with the news.

"C'mon!" I said as I punched the button again.

"Breathe," John said, gently rubbing my arms.

The elevator door opened, and I pushed my way through the crowd of people exiting. "Excuse me, excuse me, please," I pleaded. The fear that radiated through me had become a primal need to protect my baby.

We reached the NICU floor and hurried down the hall. The heavy door with the intimidating sign—NEONATAL INTEN-SIVE CARE UNIT. STERILE ENVIRONMENT. PLEASE FOLLOW PROTOCOL—was all that stood between us and our son.

I clenched my teeth and moaned at the leisurely speed at which the door opened. Once there was enough space for my body, I squeezed through. My eyes landed on Ryan's room, then shifted to the wash station. I grabbed the soap, scrubbed my hands, and pulled a sterile gown from the shelf. In my frantic state, my hands were clumsy, and the gown twisted around me.

"Dammit!" I yelled.

The frustration of our "new normal" was overpowering. I wanted to be with my baby without having to sterilize myself. This was so new, so raw. The expectations being placed upon me, as necessary as they were, were maddening.

Finally at Ryan's side, I scanned every inch of him from his head down to his toes. His eyes were closed, his body still except for the mechanical rise and fall of his chest. My breathing slowed as I studied him.

His face was angelic, innocent, perfect. Ten fingers, ten toes. Where were the signs of Down syndrome?

"This has to be a mistake," I said to John.

Our son was fighting for his life. Nine days on a ventilator with tubes, wires, and needles on every limb. Wasn't that enough for him to endure? Doctors aren't perfect. They make mistakes. Maybe this was one of those times, and the blood tests had been mixed up. It had to be some other baby—not Ryan. We hadn't been shown any proof yet, so there still was a chance they were wrong and that Ryan would be okay. Maybe my prayers had been answered.

Denial is very, very powerful.

But what if it's true? I wondered. I tried to picture him bigger. Older. What would he be like? What would life be like? Would he be happy? He would be loved. That much was certain. But how would he be treated by the rest of the world? Would he be mocked? Ridiculed? Would I be able to protect him? I had been bullied as a child, a teen, and even as an adult. What chance would Ryan have if he were disabled? All I could offer my precious baby was love. Would that be enough?

I placed my hand on his chest and felt his heart beating. I closed my eyes and counted the thumps. One, two, three, four, five, six, seven, eight, nine, ten. The rhythm calmed me, and I felt my fear lessen. *I can do this,* I thought.

A voice behind me called me from my thoughts. "Hello, Mr. and Mrs. Wilson." It was Dr. Kanton, the neonatologist. She was accompanied by a woman who she introduced as Laura, a social worker. Both of them joined us by Ryan's side.

My body stiffened as I lifted my hand from my baby's chest.

"Why don't we go talk?" Laura suggested.

My eyes stayed on Ryan and I caressed his head. "Mommy and Daddy love you so much, sweet boy. We'll be back."

We walked in silence down a long, narrow, windowless hallway surrounded by plain white walls. The doctor opened her office door and led us inside. It was cold and sterile like the NICU. Two beige chairs sat across from a beige sofa. Framed degrees, certificates, and photos covered the walls. It was so cold that I shivered.

"Are you familiar with Down syndrome?" Laura asked us.

"To an extent, yes," I said. "But not in terms of understanding it."

"Down syndrome is a genetic disorder that occurs at conception. It's caused when there is an abnormal cell division resulting in an extra chromosome, specifically chromosome 21. People with this syndrome have distinct facial characteristics and developmental delays, both physically and mentally. And in some cases, like Ryan's, a heart defect."

Realizing I was holding my breath, I forced myself to exhale. "You said this happens at conception. So, I couldn't have prevented it?" Even though I knew I'd done everything "by the book," I'd been going over and over this possibility ever since the doctor had mentioned the word *syndrome.*

"Correct. No one could have prevented this from happening."

I wanted to take comfort in her words, but as a mother, my responsibility was to protect my baby. I felt like I had already failed. I'd chosen to bring a child into this world. I'd pushed the pregnancy, desperate for it to happen after suffering an earlier miscarriage. The depth of the loss of that first baby, that excitement, that dream, was shocking. I had known some people who had miscarried and felt compassion for them, but I didn't understand the trauma until it happened to me. The combination of sorrow, anger at God, jealousy of other pregnant women, guilt because I couldn't keep my baby alive, and loneliness because my husband didn't understand, had been all-consuming. I needed a respite from all of it. The cure was another pregnancy, the creation of another dream. I left a successful career to reduce my stress to ensure that the next pregnancy would create our perfect child. That had been my plan, anyway.

But I'd been impatient. It was taking too long to get pregnant again, so we sought medical intervention. We learned that artificial insemination using my husband's sperm would increase our odds of success. And it must have been meant to be, I'd thought, because I became pregnant after the first attempt. I hadn't realized then the extent to which I was forcing life to happen on my terms instead of trusting, letting go, and believing that a net would appear. Maybe if I had just waited and let it happen naturally, we would have had a baby born full-term without a genetic defect.

I felt responsible for every bit of suffering Ryan was enduring. It was I who had brought this tiny, two-and-a-half-pound baby into a world of loud noises, tubes, needles, and horrific invasive procedures. Now he was facing the challenges of a world with an extra chromosome. I feared I would always blame myself.

"What questions do you have?" Laura asked, jolting me from my trance.

"How will he develop?" John asked.

"In Ryan's case, it's too soon to know. Our first priority is his health."

"Will he look like us?" I didn't know what to ask and immediately felt like a fool for presenting such a shallow question. I felt ashamed and looked away.

"Yes, he will have characteristics of both parents. Down syndrome children still share features of their parents, but also traits specific to the syndrome."

"What traits?"

"Facially, there's a specific shape to the eyes, like an almond, and they tend to have a flatter profile to the face with a small nose. Also, there is generally short stature and low muscle tone."

We took a long, silent moment to process.

"His heart defect," I said. "What does that mean now that we know he has Down syndrome?"

Dr. Kanton cleared her throat. "Because Ryan's lungs are so small right now, the atrial septal defect is causing his heart—and therefore his entire body—to work harder. Surgery may be needed to repair it. For now, the cardiologist will monitor him."

The social worker shifted and leaned forward. "But, if you're going to have a syndrome, be glad it's Down syndrome," she said.

"I'm sorry, what?" I said, incredulous.

"There are far worse syndromes one could have. Children with Down syndrome are very loving and sweet, so it's good that this is what your son has."

I looked at Dr. Kanton, expecting her to interrupt, but she was silent. Did she not hear what the social worker had just said, or had she chosen to ignore it? Was she lacking in compassion, or did she simply not care? If Dr. Kanton was deferring to the expertise of the social worker in knowing the best way to handle this discussion, she was mistaken.

"Here, look at this." Laura opened a photo album filled with pictures of disabled children at a camp with which she was involved and handed it to us. Most of the children had Down syndrome. We were holding our future in our hands. "See how wonderful they are?" she said with unmistakable enthusiasm as she flipped the pages.

My mouth opened to respond, but I had no words. I felt she was being insensitive. John and I were living hour by hour, learning the ins and outs of the NICU, not knowing if our baby was going to survive. I knew her positivity was meant to provide comfort, but painting a picture of rainbows and butterflies of life with a child with special needs was not the approach I needed then. This was scary, and we were sad. Acknowledging our fear and sorrow would have validated our emotions. Instead, her message indicated that we should feel grateful for our baby's circumstance. That was unrealistic. I felt unequipped on every level, especially in embracing Down syndrome. The unknowns were immense—the biggest one being: would Ryan live?

I was in a free fall, wondering where I would land. If Ryan died, would I be able to grieve two babies back-to-back? After my miscarriage, I'd taken to running in Central Park, often stopping in hidden spots to let my tears fall. Only then could I go home and pretend that I was fine. I had learned early on that my husband expected me to "just get over it."

"It's in the past," he would say. "Stop being so sad."

He'd left for work the second I returned from the doctor's office after the D&C procedure that removed the dead fetus from my uterus, leaving me to grieve alone. I knew I wouldn't have the ability to suppress my emotions and fake it this time. It wasn't just the Down syndrome diagnosis that had me feeling insecure and terrified. It was the unrealistic, unreasonable expectations that would be placed upon me. What would that mean for our marriage?

The ease with which Laura spoke about Down syndrome and the love she felt for the kids was admirable. But love takes on a whole new meaning when it's your own child facing a new world. I doubted she had considered that. We'd had a dream. Not just for ourselves, but for our child. The uncomplicated, full-term delivery of a healthy baby—a celebration filled with joy, laughter, and love. A husband and wife bonding over the miracle we'd created, our child safely at home in a peaceful environment, with opportunities to grow, to learn, to thrive. Part of that dream had been lost. Part was still possible. But the remnants of our dream had to be reconstructed with pieces of mismatched sizes and colors. The creation could turn into one of beauty or could be full of tatters. We had no way of knowing what the new dream would become. No matter how great Ryan might turn out to be, he was like a stranger to us because we didn't have knowledge of nor experience with his syndrome, much less his health issues. Before we could get to know him, we had to learn his new language.

Noticing my pained expression, Laura added, "You also have the option of putting your son up for adoption. Many parents don't feel they can handle the challenges of Down syndrome, and many others are looking to adopt these babies."

"Adoption?" I said. "No. God gave this baby to us. We love him and would never give him away."

The suggestion of adoption made it sound so easy. Just wash

your hands of your child and give him away to someone who wants him—the implication being that I didn't want him. Snap your fingers and *poof*, the problem disappears. I wouldn't consider that and couldn't see how it would solve anything. The grief would remain, and the pain would be permanent. My dream was lost, but possibilities remained. I preferred looking forward to opportunities rather than giving up. Adoption was not the answer for us. Faith was.

"How will this affect Ryan?" I asked Dr. Kanton.

"Well, in addition to the heart defect, children with Down syndrome also tend to have weakened immune systems, so he's more susceptible to becoming ill. That presents a greater risk in his current state as a preemie with a compromised respiratory system."

"So are you saying that he now has an even greater chance of dying?"

"It's possible, yes," she said. "He has a long road ahead and a long way to go before he's out of the woods. It's best to not get ahead of yourself. While the Down syndrome diagnosis is a big part of who your son will be, it's a small piece of the puzzle. Getting him bigger and stronger is our focal point, because if that doesn't happen, the syndrome will not matter."

While I appreciated her words, as a mother, all pieces were all-encompassing, and I didn't have the ability to compartmentalize my child. I decided I'd heard enough. "Let's go back to Ryan," I told John.

Depleted, we said our thanks and left.

The nurse was finishing changing Ryan's diaper when we walked in. "He's doing a bit better today," she told us. "Would you like to hold him?"

That single question gave me an unexpected surge of hope. I had waited nine days for this moment. Now not only could I tell Ryan that I loved him, but he would actually feel it from the warmth of my skin, from my breathing, from my heartbeat.

"Oh, my God, can I?"

The nurse nodded, carefully detangling his tubes and wires before gingerly placing him in my arms. The comfort of being able to hold Ryan for the first time invigorated me. At that moment, his warmth pushed away some of my apprehension for his future.

Pressed up against my chest, his eyes opened ever so slightly. I felt his vulnerability, as if he were asking, "Am I safe?"

"Hello, my beautiful son." I smiled and kissed his head. "Mommy and Daddy are here, Ryan. You have nothing to worry about."

I held him like he was a fragile bird with a broken wing, terrified of moving the wrong way, causing him pain, or dislodging one of the tubes or wires.

"You're doing great," said his nurse. "He's safe in your arms. Just relax."

I began rocking him. With his head against my breast, I could feel the milk surging in anticipation of release. *Can he feel it?* I wondered. I had been pumping and freezing my breast milk since he'd been born, hoping that one day he would be able to drink it. Maybe this closeness gave him a sense of familiarity with me as his mom.

Looking up at John, I asked him, "Do you think he knows who we are?"

"I'm sure he does."

God, I hope so, I thought.

"Do you recognize my voice, Ryan? I'm your mommy. I love you with all of my heart." I hoped that when he looked at me, he saw only my love and not my fear.

By the end of that day, I learned that polar opposite emotions can exist within a relationship at any given moment. Not quite like a love/hate relationship, but more of an "I'm so grateful you are in my life but am terrified of having you in my life." Also: "I love you with all my heart but feel sad when looking at you." As a mother, those are tough thoughts to embrace.

I had grown up with a mom whose life didn't allow her the ability to love unconditionally. She had been abused by her parents. When she grew up, she married my dad, an alcoholic who left her alone with three young children and provided no spousal or child support, and whose idea of time spent with his children was taking them to a local bar where he could drink with his friends while his four, six, and eight-year-old children ate peanuts and played pool and shuffleboard. We were innocent victims of their dysfunction.

My mom often told me that I was an extreme disappointment. She would shame me in front of others by forcing me to show the welts she'd left upon my legs, arms, or back with the belt she used to "teach me a lesson."

"I hate you," she'd often tell me. But the most impactful words she had ever said to me were, "I hope you have children as rotten as you are."

As a child, I vowed that if I were one day blessed enough to have children, I would cherish them, love them unconditionally, and express gratitude every day for the privilege of being their mother. This caused my feelings of sadness over Ryan's fate to clash with the lessons I had learned from being a child myself, and the promise I'd made to my future self and my future children.

I knew it would take time to work through the emotional conflict. I also knew that I possessed an unshakable love and resolve to protect my son. That was my truth, and it is what carried me through the astonishing reactions of friends and family over the course of many days.

After the Down syndrome diagnosis was shared, it became evident that dealing with societal distress would be a difficult endeavor. Hearts were in the right place, but heads were not. Including my own.

The afternoon of the diagnosis, I stood dazedly staring out the large picture window in our living room. I called Megan.

"How's Ryan today?" she asked me. "Did you get the results?"

"Honestly, I'm afraid to say it out loud," I told her.

"Do you want me to come over?"

"No." Tears raced down my face. "I just wanted to let you know that Ryan has Down syndrome."

"Oh, Susan. I'm so sorry!"

After a long silence and with a quivering chin, I said, "Will you still be my friend?"

"Oh, my God, what? Of course, I will! Why would you ask me that?"

"Because I'm scared. I don't know how friends and family will react. What if they're afraid and walk away? What if they don't want to know Ryan?"

"Why would you think that?" Megan asked.

"My own dad walked away from three healthy children. What if they leave me like my dad did?"

"Oh, sweetie, here is what I know," Megan said. "Your dad is an ass and a coward. You are an amazing person and now will be an amazing mom to your beautiful baby boy. And I am here for you no matter what. And anyone who dares walk away…well, you don't need them in your life, and neither does Ryan."

"Thank you. I can't wait for you to meet my son."

I tensed up every time the phone rang because I never knew what I would hear on the other end.

"Oh, my God, is it true?" asked a friend, a mother herself, who called to find out.

I held the phone, stunned. "Yes, our baby has Down syndrome." Hearing the horror in her voice validated my fears about how the world would treat my son. It also strengthened my resolve to safeguard him. "But," I added, "he's amazing. I got to hold him today for the first time."

"Oh, gosh, you must be so sad."

"It was a shock, but he's a beautiful little boy, and I'm so blessed to be his mom." Her suggestion of my sadness made me fight it all the more.

"Well, wow, that's great, then," she replied without conviction.

My mother-in-law didn't call for three days. Why wasn't she reaching out? I was closer to her than I was to my own mom. She was the sweetest, most caring woman on earth. Did she not want to be a grandmother to a child with Down syndrome? That had to be an irrational thought, I told myself, but it did cross my mind. In the midst of my pain, what I didn't appreciate was that she was reacting like a mother herself. Her heart was breaking for her grandson and for her own child—my husband, John—

just like my heart was breaking for Ryan. She needed time, just like I did.

Then one day, my friend Mary called. "Congratulations!" she exclaimed.

"You're the only person who's said that to me. Thank you for that." I was lifted by that one simple word. Nobody had even once congratulated me on Ryan's birth once the Down syndrome became known.

"Of course!" Mary said. "You have a beautiful baby boy! How are you holding up?"

"Obviously not what we were expecting, but he's so beautiful. But also very sick, so we don't know what to expect."

"If there was ever a parent that this little boy should be sent to, it's you."

That simple conversation filled my heart with love and confidence. It was the first time since Ryan's birth that my smile wasn't forced or mixed with fear. To this day, I consider Mary's perspective, her sincerity, and her love one of the greatest gifts I received.

Having just finished a crash course in neonates, we next got a crash course in Down syndrome. Determined to help our child reach the stars, we researched everything, including the characteristics of this syndrome, ranges of developmental delays, early intervention programs for babies and children, and other common medical issues that Ryan could face.

Leaders of the early intervention programs welcomed us with unexpected love and compassion. They knew what was ahead of us better than anyone else. We needed them, and Ryan needed their expertise. They were committed to helping us when our son was ready. For the first time, I didn't feel so lost.

Eleven days after his birth, Ryan was finally ready to breathe without help from the ventilator. My prayers were so close to being answered. With the removal of the breathing tube came the removal of the adhesives and coverings around his mouth, allowing us to see his entire face for the first time. With his lips slightly parted, his eyes searched our faces as we smiled at him.

"Hi, Ryan," I said as I gently caressed my baby's cheeks with my hand, touching the skin that had been revealed.

What does he feel? I wondered.

My spirits soared as I held him. He felt less encumbered. Or maybe I did.

One step closer to recovery, I thought, feeling elated.

For the next several weeks, my days were spent at Ryan's side. Every morning, I walked into that hospital with a purpose, focused on the most important mission of my life: assuring my son that he was loved. Friends would ask me out to lunch, but there was no place I would rather be than with Ryan.

As he grew, I grew. I prayed more. I became more grateful for the little things, the things that I had taken for granted. I learned that I had the capacity to love absolutely. I learned that it was okay to be afraid and that I was strong and courageous with astounding determination. I learned who I was because of my son. That was the first of many gifts Ryan gave to me.

Chapter Three

"He's not out of the woods," was Dr. Kanton's daily declaration during those first few weeks. She didn't want us to get our hopes up, but I yearned for hope. Hope was what got me out of bed. It was what propelled me forward each day.

"But it must be a good sign that he's still alive and off the ventilator, isn't it?" I would ask her.

"It's one step forward, two steps back. The fact that Ryan is still alive means he's a fighter, but he's a very sick baby and at high risk for infection and setbacks. He will need additional blood transfusions and has a long way to go before he's out of the woods."

Her continual imagery of my baby being in "the woods" was distressing. To me, the woods represented darkness, fear, and vulnerability. I envisioned a barely visible trail with hazardous impediments: broken branches and sharp stones, sounds of wolves howling, and unknown threats lingering behind tree trunks waiting to pounce on the unsuspecting traveler.

Ryan was on a bumpy path, and something unseen could

creep in and attack him, but he was being cared for by a highly specialized medical team and protected by two parents who would walk through fire for him. He had help navigating through those dark woods. Wasn't that enough to protect him?

Ryan's progress in week three proved my point. The nasal cannula, which provided him with supplemental oxygen, and the nasogastric tube feeding him were removed. For the first time, his face was free of tubes, and his body was free of invasive treatments. I began to embrace the dream of taking my baby home and being a mom.

"Would you like to feed him his first bottle?" the nurse asked me.

"Yes!" I exclaimed as my forehead wrinkled in surprise. "Oh, my gosh, really?"

The nurse smiled. "Really."

Sunshine flooded my soul. "Did you hear that, Ryan? Mommy's going to feed you a bottle!"

Grinning from ear to ear, I looked down at his sweet angelic face, elation surging through me. I readied myself in the rocking chair as the nurse placed his little bundled body in my lap, positioning his head in the crook of my arm.

I yearned to have my baby at my breast, but he wasn't strong enough and couldn't handle the volume of milk that would be released. The tiny preemie bottle held just a teaspoon of my breast milk, but the simple act of feeding it to him made me feel like a real mom. I beamed, watching his tiny lips purse to suckle the nipple as he made a sweet squeaky noise. I was such a proud mama when he accomplished that! It was also the first real accomplishment that I had felt as his mother.

Each subsequent day brought much-needed hope and a

feeling that a miracle was on the horizon. Ryan was not just still alive but also growing ounces at a time. Before we knew it, he was up to three pounds and looking less like a fragile bird. It seemed he had found his way out of the woods.

I spent the days rocking him, feeding him, talking to him, sharing dreams, and expressing my love. He may not have been able to understand me, but I knew he could hear me by the way his tiny eyes were laser-focused on mine as I spoke.

"You are going to have a magical life filled with love and laughter. You will play with Jake, who, by the way, will love you to pieces! You will have friends. You will pick apples off a tree and pumpkins from a field. You will feel the sand between your toes and the sunshine on your face. You will learn how to throw and kick a ball. You will run around searching for Easter eggs, and you will put the angel on top of the Christmas tree. There is nothing you won't be able to do."

The more often I said those words, the more deeply I felt them to be true. And I knew that one day, Ryan would feel it too. On other days, I'd tell him all about his family—his grandparents, aunts and uncles, and cousins—and how excited everyone was to meet him. Pictures of our family decorated the sides of his incubator.

"Look, Ryan. This is Mommy and Daddy, and this is Jake." I pointed to each picture, knowing he couldn't understand, not even knowing if he could even see the pictures. But it didn't matter. I felt better knowing that our faces were there when we couldn't be.

Sometimes, family members would visit us through the NICU window, and I would wave and point to Ryan. Encouraged by my happy enthusiasm, they smiled, optimistic that they would one day be able to meet him.

"Aunt Paula is waving to you, Ryan. She's right there at the window. She loves you so much and can't wait to hold you." He couldn't give her the smile she wished for, but I could as I waved back to my sister.

As Ryan and I sat together each day, his tiny head lying on my chest, our bond strengthened and became a force. It was as if my blood was pumping through him as I held him—an invisible umbilical cord giving him strength.

With each sliver of improvement in Ryan's health, I felt that I was holding tomorrow in my arms. This allowed me to go home every night feeling hopeful and looking forward to the next day. The more days passed, the closer we were to bringing our baby home. Every twenty-four-hour period became a gift.

On the first day of week four, I was packing my bag for the day at the hospital when the phone rang.

"Mrs. Wilson?" came the voice on the line.

"Yes."

"Good morning. This is Meredith, Ryan's nurse."

My shoulders slumped as I put my bag down. Why would she be calling unless it was bad news?

"Is Ryan okay?" I asked.

"Yes," she said, "he's doing well. I'm calling with good news! Ryan has been moved to our step-down unit. I wanted you to know where to go before you come in this morning."

"Oh, that is the best news! Thank you!" I said, exhaling in relief.

She told me where to go and added, "If you have clothing for him, like onesies or pajamas, bring them, because you can dress him."

I hung up the phone and crossed my hands over my heart, thanking God. The corners of my mouth spread to my ears as I ran up the stairs to the room that would soon be Ryan's nursery. I grabbed a shopping bag and filled it with the preemie clothing we'd bought.

The step-down unit was where preemies went when they no longer needed critical care. The doctor had said it could happen but didn't say when, and I hadn't known it would happen so soon. We were one step closer to bringing our baby home.

I blasted the car radio as I made the twenty-minute drive to the hospital, singing freely, my fingers tapping to the beat on the steering wheel, windows down, the breeze blowing in. I stopped at a red light and became aware of the driver in the car next to me staring at me in amusement. I smiled and continued to use my fingers as drumsticks. The joy that had taken a temporary hiatus was now back in my heart. I had forgotten what it was like to simply feel happy, and I embraced the ease of how life now felt.

The bright sun radiating down that day was no match for the smile on my face, and the mood was different as I entered the NICU—lighter. I felt my hope sweep across the room. I sensed joy, which I imagined the nurses must have needed just as much as the parents. It dawned on me that I hadn't had time to consider how the medical staff must have felt taking care of sick babies, seeing them suffer, watching parents cry—sometimes witnessing life draining from the babies, knowing dreams were dying and parents' hearts were breaking. Until that moment, I hadn't appreciated the fact that transferring a preemie to the step-down unit was a "win" for the staff. The care they provided was to make these preemies stronger, opening a window for possibilities and hope for the day these teeny, tiny gifts from God got better and moved on. They craved this progress, and all of our lives depended on it.

"Hi, Mrs. Wilson," a nurse said with a smile. "Ryan is just down to the left."

"Thank you!"

Ryan's new room was just a few doors down from his old one, but it was like being in a different building. *Wow,* I thought as I stopped and stood in the doorway, taking it all in. Ryan was one of four babies in the room. Each baby was in a bassinet. It was quiet, calm, and there was a window looking out onto a courtyard. Ryan was asleep, and he looked peaceful and serene. No loud beeps, no bright lights. This was a little bit of heaven just feet from what seemed like hell.

Ryan had graduated to the status of a "grower and feeder." His only job now was to eat and gain weight. My job was to become an active participant in my son's care to prepare me for bringing him home.

The step-down unit provided me with the opportunity to stay with Ryan and care for him without interruptions and noise. I was afraid at first, nervous I would do something wrong that could harm him. After watching your baby on the brink of death, with tubes and wires everywhere, it takes time to transition from the emotional trauma to a place of comfort and confidence. But I adapted to this new environment and embraced my new responsibility. I was proud of my baby boy, and of his strength and determination to live Ryan was my inspiration.

With each passing day, I came to know my son simply by caring for him; from the straightforward acts of diaper changing and feeding him a bottle to recognizing his cries and figuring out what he needed. I didn't realize it then, but the most important thing I learned was to recognize his energy level—his "baseline." I was Ryan's one daily constant, so I was able to tell when he was having a good day or seemed a bit off. Just like a typical mother-child relationship.

A few days in, as I sat rocking and feeding Ryan, a new baby was brought in. He was accompanied by a tall, dark, handsome man in scrubs—so attractive that I did a double take. *Who's that doctor? He's so handsome! Too bad he's not Ryan's doctor,* I thought, secretly chuckling.

I learned quickly that he was the new father of twins who had been born prematurely that morning—a boy and a girl. The girl was smaller, requiring oxygen, so she was in the critical care area. The boy was able to breathe on his own, so he immediately became a "grower and feeder." Later that day the new mom was wheeled in to see her son. The expression on her face reminded me of my own the night Ryan was born. Her eyebrows were lowered, her lower lip was protruding, and tears welled in her eyes. As she brought her hand up to her face, I could feel her sadness and fear.

The mom's name was Regina. She was petite and pretty with wild black hair and dark eyes. She and her husband were an attractive couple, the kind that would turn heads on a street. Regina's husband rested his hands tenderly on her shoulders as they listened to the doctor explain their son's condition. I admired his strength and his presence at his wife's side.

A few days later, Regina's baby girl joined her baby brother as a grower and feeder. Regina and I shared that room with a quiet desperation for our children to be okay. We hadn't yet spoken but simply nodded hello upon arriving, both of us pumping our breast milk to feed to our babies via a preemie bottle. We gave our bottles to the nurses, who then stored them in a refrigerator until it was feeding time.

"If you're ready to feed Ryan, I'll go get your bottle from the fridge," Ryan's nurse, Annie, said to me.

I nodded and picked Ryan up, smiling down at him as he nestled into me. "Are you ready to eat?"

Annie returned with my bottle and put it on the shelf in a container of warm water. Then she said, "I'll be right back," and left the room.

As I sat cradling Ryan, rocking back and forth, I looked up and saw that the bottle was suddenly gone. *Where is it?* I wondered.

When Annie returned, she went for the bottle and found it missing. A nervous look crossed her face as she turned and whispered to Kathy, the other nurse. Both cast a glance at Regina, who was feeding her daughter a bottle.

"Did you give my breast milk to the other baby?" I asked Kathy, my eyebrows raised. At this, Regina's eyes widened as she looked first to me and then to the nurses.

"I'm so sorry, Mrs. Wilson," Annie said. "Kathy picked up your bottle thinking it belonged to the other mom."

Regina jerked the bottle from her baby's mouth and held it like it was about to explode. Kathy swiftly grabbed it.

My emotions weren't exactly steady at that point, and all I could think of was what Ryan was going to eat now. It wasn't a rational thought, given that they had more of my frozen breast milk stored and my breasts still had plenty of milk to pump— but in that moment, being understanding wasn't an option.

Not wanting Ryan to sense my distress, I gently placed him

in his bassinet and walked to the door, motioning for Annie to follow me. "How could that happen?" I hissed under my breath. "My bottle has my name on it! Her baby was drinking *my* breast milk!"

"I know, and I'm sorry. Kathy made a mistake."

"That's a big mistake. Now what?"

"I'll get another bottle warmed and will be right back so that you can feed Ryan," Annie said. "We'll discuss this later if that's okay with you?"

Do I have a choice? I wondered. Exhaling loudly, I went back to Ryan and noticed that Regina was gone. Once again cradling my baby in my arms, I massaged his feet while we waited for another bottle.

"You'll eat soon, beautiful boy."

Ryan was calm. His brown, almond-shaped eyes stared up at me as if reassuring me that everything was okay.

An hour later, after feeding him and settling him in for a nap, I curled up in the rocking chair by the window with a trashy romance novel, happy to be transported to a place of perfect love in a perfect world.

My mind drifted to the day when Ryan would be home and we could begin our journey as a family, with my husband doting on us both. I knew it would not be without challenges. John and I were new parents overcoming a traumatic premature birth, and we still had much to learn about the world of Down syndrome. But Ryan's "birth defect," as it was called, was not a defect in our eyes. It was an opportunity to open our hearts to a person and to a world that was unexpected. I'd be lying if I said I wasn't afraid. I was terrified. And I was sad. But I can also say that the love I felt for my son and the grace given to me by family and friends helped me to push through the trepidation and sorrow. This little boy was beautiful, and he was a gift from God. As long as Ryan was alive, my heart would be whole, and we would be okay.

Staring out at the courtyard, lost in my thoughts, I was jolted back to reality when Annie came in. "Mrs. Wilson," she said, "may Kathy and I speak with you outside for a moment?"

Still a bit irritated at Kathy and not thrilled to be interrupted and taken from my happy place, I put my book down. Not wanting to leave Ryan's side, I made sure he was still in my line of sight as I stood just outside the doorway.

"I'm so sorry, Mrs. Wilson. I promise you it will not happen again," Kathy insisted.

"I appreciate that, but I don't understand how it could happen at all."

"The other mother would like to speak with you. Since her baby drank your milk, she has some questions to ask you."

"What do you mean?" I asked, my brows creased.

"Well, she's concerned about what her baby may have ingested."

I turned from Kathy to Annie, my mouth agape.

"She'd like to know if anything harmful could be in your breast milk," Annie clarified.

"Of course there's nothing harmful in my milk!" I said indignantly.

"She just wants to be sure. Will you speak with her?"

"Wait," I said, "let me get this straight. You give her baby my milk and I'm the one who has to answer questions?"

"Please Mrs. Wilson," Annie said.

Angrily, I responded, "Yes, I will talk to her and alleviate her concerns."

I turned and went back to Ryan. I held him tightly until I left for home. All I wanted to do was protect him. I especially hated the thought of leaving him that night. While my baby wasn't hurt that day, someone else's could have been. What if my breast milk had been tainted with drugs or alcohol? For Regina, there was no knowing what was in it. As incensed as I was at Kathy's mistake, I couldn't help but wonder how Regina must have felt, worrying about what might be in her baby's system. I felt compassion for her, but I also experienced my first feeling of doubt about the care my baby was receiving. If such a potentially harmful mistake could be made in what should be a simple process, what else could happen?

For the first time, I realized that the hospital staff—especially the nurses, since they were the ones with my baby ninety-nine percent of the time—were fallible and made mistakes just like the rest of us. But with a life at stake, was it too much for a parent to expect them to be better? I knew that the majority of the hospital staff was competent and dedicated, but the negligence displayed on that day opened a floodgate of anxiety and the realization that the sooner I could get my baby home, the better.

Regina approached me as I was packing up to head home. "Hi," she said, "can we talk for a minute?"

"Yes, of course," I said, forcing a half smile as I set my bag down.

"I'm so sorry to ask you this, and I mean no offense, but are there any drugs or alcohol in your breast milk, or are you taking any type of medication?" Her eyebrows were raised and her eyes were wide, as if pleading for me to say no.

"No," I said. "There's nothing harmful in my system that could have been transmitted through my breast milk. I would never do that to my baby." I looked down at Ryan, my hand resting on his head. "I realize you don't know me and all you have are my words, but I promise, you have nothing to worry about."

"Thank you. The nurses reassured me of that also, since they've seen you with your baby, but I needed to ask." She smiled, and I could feel her sense of relief.

Exhausted, I said goodbye to Ryan and good night to Regina. On my way out, I stopped at the nurse's desk to speak to Annie. "I know it's not your fault," I said, "but today left me feeling worried about Ryan's care. Not from you, but in general. Can you please make sure the night nurse is aware and takes extra precautions to be sure he's safe?"

"Of course, Mrs. Wilson," Annie said. "Try not to worry. Go home and get some sleep."

Not worry? Impossible.

There's that old saying: *What you don't know can't hurt you.* Well, it actually can hurt you, but you just don't know it. In this instance, the breast milk debacle caused my trust in the system to falter. Like a vase that shatters, making it almost impossible to put it back together and have it look and feel the way it did before.

This was just one example of the risks of having a premature baby who required special care. There were simply too many caregivers with opportunities to negatively affect my baby's health. With preemies, we moms go into this blind, so to speak. We are innocents ourselves, with no knowledge of the world we're in, trying to protect our most precious possession, our baby, with no weapons, armor, or knowledge of the enemy we face. We're shooting in the dark, blindfolded, dependent on verbal cues that aren't in our vocabulary. To survive, trust is a prerequisite. But what happens when that trust is broken? Fear and anxiety return, invading the faith and positivity that had temporarily taken hold.

When I walked into Ryan's room the next morning, Regina was holding her daughter. She smiled cautiously at me. Sensing her uncertainty and hoping to put her at ease, I asked, "How are your babies today?"

"They're doing really well," she said, her smile growing as she looked down at her daughter's face.

In that moment, I saw us as two mothers with the same goal: loving and protecting our babies.

Regina stood and placed her baby back in her bed. "I'm going to get a cup of coffee. Would you like something?"

"Mmm, yes, I'd love one, thank you," I said and reached for my purse to get money, but Regina shook her head.

"No, please let me."

I smiled and nodded, accepting the olive branch extended.

Over the next few days, Regina and I were like two moms on a playdate, holding our babies, sharing stories over coffee, and laughing. It felt almost like normal. *Almost.* Regina's twins were getting bigger and healthier by the day, and Ryan was right behind them. Soon, I thought, we would be having playdates at home.

Dr. Kanton surprised me at the beginning of week five when she informed me that Ryan was going to be turned over to the care of a pediatrician John and I had selected.

"Is that safe?" I asked her.

"It's important for Ryan's pediatrician to get to know him before he's discharged, so he'll be stopping in each day to check on him. I'll be available if needed."

"Are you sure Ryan is ready?" I asked her. As much as I wanted that next step to happen, I felt anxious about it. Ryan was only five weeks old and still just over three pounds.

"Your baby has made great progress. I assure you this is an appropriate and timely transition."

I nodded. "Okay, if that's what you feel is best."

Two days later, I noticed that a pulse oximeter had been brought back to Ryan's room for oxygen monitoring purposes. When I asked why, Annie told me that Dr. Kanton had ordered it.

I asked the nurse to elaborate but she couldn't, so she called the pediatrician. I spoke to him over the phone and he told me the pulse oximeter was not necessary and ordered it pulled.

When I arrived at the hospital the next morning, Ryan seemed tired, not himself. He was pale and didn't want to take a bottle, becoming more lethargic as the day wore on. Before leaving for the night, I brought it to Annie's attention.

"Ryan seems off," I said. "Almost weak. I feel like I should stay with him."

"He definitely hasn't been himself today," she said. "Go home and get some rest. It's six o'clock and you've been here all day. I'll keep a close eye on him and will let the night nurse know."

I nodded tentatively. "I'll see you tomorrow, Ryan. I love you," I said, caressing his head as he slept.

I hated leaving him that night. To this day, I wish I hadn't. But that was part of the drill of having a baby in the NICU. You eventually had to go home.

Our phone rang at four o'clock in the morning, startling us awake. I raised myself onto my elbow, rubbing my eyes as John sleepily answered the phone.

"Who is it?" I asked him.

He held his finger up as he listened to the person on the other end. "Okay," he said. "I understand. We'll be there soon."

"What's going on?" I asked.

"That was the hospital. Ryan crashed in the middle of the night. He stopped breathing and is back on life support."

"*No!*" I cried as I drew my knees to my chest in a fetal position and wept.

Chapter Four

The visual was heartbreaking: Ryan back on life support, heavily sedated and in a paralytic state, naked but for his diaper, looking as fragile as he had the day he was born. The ventilator tube was back, taped securely around his mouth, and a feeding tube had been inserted into his nose. Wires once again covered his body, and here he was, just steps away from where he had been thriving only thirty-six hours earlier.

I touched his cheek, my hand trembling. "Mommy's here, Ryan," I whispered. I turned to John. "I knew I shouldn't have left him last night. I knew he wasn't himself." My face twisted with pain and guilt. "Maybe this wouldn't have happened if I'd stayed."

"This isn't your fault," John said. "What could you have done differently to change the outcome?"

"I know it's not my fault, but clearly the nurse wasn't as attentive as she should have been, or else Ryan wouldn't have stopped breathing! And at least I would have been with him."

"Susan, you can't stay here 24/7."

"Why not?" I shot back, my eyes black with anger.

"Good morning," Ryan's nurse said as she came to our sides.

My eyes shifted from John to the face of yet another stranger caring for my son. "What happened?" I asked her.

All she said was, "The doctor will be in soon to speak with you."

"Do you know what caused this?"

Again, she only said, "The doctor will explain everything as soon as she arrives."

"Why can't you just tell me?" I demanded through a clenched jaw. "I need to know why this happened, when less than twenty-four hours ago, he was just across this room, breathing on his own. What the hell happened?"

"I can't say. You will have to wait for the doctor."

Raw anger shot through me as I glared at the nurse. "My baby almost died, again, and you *can't say?*"

"I'm sorry," she said, then turned away.

As I stood shaking, staring at Ryan's motionless body, John put his arm around my waist and said, "I need to get to the office."

"Can't you stay until we speak with the doctor?" I begged, tears in my eyes. "Please don't leave. Please!"

"I'm sorry, I have early meetings this morning." He hugged me tightly and kissed my cheek. "Keep me posted."

My blood began to boil as he left, the heat rising to my face. It was as if my tears had turned into lava, sending streams of fire down my cheeks. Even with the multitude of hospital staff swarming around, I felt alone and abandoned.

I sat at Ryan's side for hours, eyes fixed on the rhythmic rise and fall of his chest, silently pleading with God to let him live, interrupted only by the nurse periodically coming to check his vitals and draw blood.

It was just after 9 a.m. when I heard a voice in the hallway greeting the staff. Looking up, I saw Regina's beautiful, smiling face as she walked past, unaware that Ryan and I were once again residing in this open expanse of critically ill babies.

"Regina," I called out.

She stopped, taken aback. She saw me and her mouth opened. When she saw Ryan, she gasped. "Oh, Susan, what happened?"

She rushed toward me and I fell apart. Gut-wrenching sobs tore through my body.

"It's okay," Regina said, putting her arms around me, cradling my head against her shoulder.

For the protection of the preemies, admission into the NICU was strictly limited to the baby's parents. Other family members and friends could "visit" through a sound-proof window, creating the aura of lost souls in a fishbowl for those on the inside. The only source of emotional support a parent had within those walls was their spouse. In their absence, you had no choice but to face the fear, frustration, grief, guilt, and feelings of failure alone. The isolation was profound. But if you were there long enough, you might develop a bond with another parent who walked alongside you through the darkness. Regina was my light on that dark path.

Whimpering, I pulled away and wiped my face with my sleeve. "I'm sorry," I said, looking at Regina through misty eyes.

"You have nothing to apologize for!" she said. "I'm just so sad for you. What happened?"

"The nurse won't tell me, which is bullshit!" I hissed. "Apparently, only the doctor is allowed to tell me why my child almost died last night. Can you believe that? I'd love to know how they'd feel if this was happening to their child!"

Her eyes grew wide. "That's crazy!" She looked around. "Where's John?"

"He needed to get to work." I lowered my head, ashamed and livid. How could he have left me like this? Regina squeezed my hand. "I'll be okay," I said. "Go be with your babies. We can talk more later."

I was emotionally exhausted by the time Dr. Kanton arrived an hour later. "At some point within these last few days," she said, "Ryan became severely anemic. He also has pneumonia in both lungs, most likely from aspirating while feeding."

I pressed my fingers to my temples, struggling to ease the dull throbbing in my head as I tried to process what the doctor was telling me. "What does aspirating mean?" I asked.

"Aspiration is when fluid accidentally gets into a person's lungs. Because Ryan was so tired due to the anemia, he most likely couldn't swallow correctly, thereby inhaling the breast milk and causing a lung infection."

"Oh, God," I whispered. "He's still so small. Can he recover from this?"

"We don't know. It will be hour by hour. I'll check back later."

She started to leave, but I stopped her. "Wait. Two days ago, I was talking to the pediatrician about when Ryan would need another blood transfusion. He said it wasn't necessary, but clearly it was. How could he not know that Ryan was anemic? If he had, this wouldn't have happened, right?"

"I can't speak to that," the doctor said, "but I can say that we are doing everything we can to save your son."

I sat back, exhaled loudly, and shook my head. "I appreciate that, but we both know that this shouldn't have happened!"

"The pediatrician has been informed and will be in to speak with you," she said. Then she put her hand on my shoulder and left.

A silent scream of fury shrilled in my head. I was enraged. I didn't have the slightest idea what to do or say. The mood in the NICU seemed to have transformed. It almost felt as if the staff was avoiding us. Aside from a nurse coming over to monitor Ryan's vitals and draw blood, they were absent.

I sat beside Ryan, unmoving, unconsciously matching my breaths to the movements of his chest. In, out, in, out, in, out. If I could have breathed for him, I would have.

When the pediatrician finally stopped by, I was in the same stooped-over state, numb from all that had happened. I heard his footsteps and hesitated before I lifted my head. He stood at my side, looking at my son.

"Should you have ordered a blood transfusion?" I asked.

"Probably so," he said. "Hindsight is twenty-twenty." He shifted his gaze to mine. "Your son will be back under the care of Dr. Kanton for now."

What a cavalier response, I thought. No apology. No emotion. His disregard for my very sick baby confused me. Did he not care? Was my baby no more than just a chart to him, and I just another mom? Could he not see the pain etched on my face, or was he simply looking past it?

I turned those thoughts back onto myself. Had I expected too much, choosing to see him as a man in addition to a physician—a human being with a heart? Maybe I wasn't being fair to the process or to him. I wasn't a doctor or a nurse. I didn't have the knowledge required to diagnose a condition. And in that moment, I didn't have the confidence to question him further. I felt intimidated and submitted to my weakness.

Two days later, Ryan's ventilator settings were reduced from "control" to "assist," which meant that he was starting to take breaths on his own in between the breaths the machine provided. It was a sign that he was fighting.

On day three, Ryan was disconnected from the ventilator, finally able to take breaths on his own but requiring supplemental oxygen through a nasal cannula to ensure there was adequate oxygen circulating within his blood. I didn't understand much of the medical jargon at that point, but I knew it meant he was no longer in critical condition. When Ryan opened his eyes on that third day, I felt we both could breathe again.

"Hi there," I smiled as my hand gently caressed his head.

I couldn't identify what I saw in his eyes. Was it pain? Confusion? Relief? Maybe the fear of the unknown? Could a baby feel any of those things? Or could it have been that his eyes were simply mirroring my own? He stared intently at me, and it was as if through his beautiful brown almond-shaped eyes he was saying, "It's okay, Mommy. I'm not as fragile as I look."

As a result of this last intubation, Ryan was diagnosed with bronchopulmonary dysplasia, a chronic lung disease caused by lung and airway damage due to the use of forced mechanical ventilation.

It was distressing news, especially when we were told that there was no cure, but the assurance that Ryan could outgrow the disease gave us hope. Until that time, however, he would be dependent on the nasal tube for oxygen support. He would also be dependent on a nasal feeding tube until he was strong enough to resume bottle feeding. All because a pediatrician had been careless.

Dr. Kanton dropped this news on us like it was just another day at the office, seemingly oblivious to the bomb she'd just detonated. Fortunately, at that moment, I was oblivious to the debris field that lay ahead.

John spent his days at work while I spent mine at Ryan's side, showering him with love and assurances that everything would be okay. Having been brought up by a single mom who worked full time, I wanted to be a stay-at-home mom, readily available to kiss boo-boos and give hugs on demand. John made this possible, and I was grateful. Since Ryan's birth, we had instinctively fallen into our roles with a heightened sense of urgency. John worked his ass off to maintain job security and health care coverage, and I gave every bit of strength and energy I had to our son.

Sometimes, John would visit Ryan after work. On other evenings, he relied on me to communicate information and updates on Ryan's condition. On weekends, we visited the hospital together, but the visits were often short because there were always things to be done at home and John didn't like being in the hospital for extended periods of time.

The nurses encouraged me to spend time with John away from the hospital, but being apart from Ryan felt unnatural and caused me immense sadness. I felt like a tug-of-war rope, my duties as a mother and a wife being tested in a game of strength. But in this game, there was no winner.

Regina checked in on me during the week, and we'd often grab a coffee or a quick lunch in the cafeteria. Neither of us wanted to be away from our babies for very long but acknowledged our need to take a break.

Finally, the day came when Regina learned her babies were ready to go home. "I feel sad leaving you here," she told me.

I saw the pained expression on her face and my heart sank to my stomach. I'd known this day would come, and I'd tried to prepare for it, but I wasn't ready to face the days in the NICU without her. Who would I laugh and commiserate with? I took a deep breath, appreciating the gift of having Regina as a friend during the happy and dire days, understanding that it was time for her family to move on.

"I'll miss you horribly, but I'm happy for you. Get out of this place!" I gave her a smile and a hug, wishing desperately that we could leave with them.

As Ryan remained "stable" and resumed bottle feedings, conversations were had about next steps. To bring Ryan home, I needed nursing skills. I had to learn how to operate a pulse oximeter machine. I had to learn to monitor his oxygenation rates. I had to use a stethoscope to listen to his lungs to ensure there were no wheezing or crackling sounds. And I had to be able to recognize the visual signs of respiratory distress: retractions in his chest and nasal flaring. How does a new mom do that? By praying that determination, focus, and faith outweigh the giant vat of apprehension.

Laura, the social worker, checked in on us periodically throughout our weeks in the NICU, inquiring about my relationship with John, my feelings about having a baby with Down syndrome, and my readiness to be the mom of a chronically ill baby. She was always eager to offer advice. Thinking she was there simply to offer support, I was an open book, sharing every thought, fact, and fear with her.

"You're here alone so much of the time," she asked me. "How does that feel?"

"I miss my husband and I miss the time we used to spend together, but it will be better once Ryan comes home."

"Do you feel capable of providing Ryan with what he'll need, both medically and developmentally?"

I asked her what she meant.

"Well," she said, "it's scary for most moms to bring home a healthy baby, so I just want to make sure you know what to expect in caring for a baby with a chronic lung disease on top of his Down syndrome diagnosis."

"I don't think I can know what to expect," I said, "and that's a bit scary. Having a sick child with special needs was obviously not our plan, but John and I have done a lot of research on Down syndrome and are more than ready to bring our baby home and be a family." I smiled down at Ryan as I held his tiny hand.

"Will John be around? Will he be able to offer you and Ryan the support you'll need?"

I cocked my head and sighed. "Not as much as I would like, but there's not much we can do about that. He has to go to work."

Laura studied my face. "Your strength throughout this entire ordeal has been admirable. I just want to be sure you're prepared."

"I think I am. At least I will be." I wiped at the corner of my eye before she could see the tear.

After weeks of concentrated training with the nurses and a total of ten weeks in the NICU, Ryan was ready. But Laura and Dr. Kanton threw us a bottom-of-the-ninth curve ball by recommending an "adjustment period" at a nearby chronic care children's hospital. The aim was for us to get "more comfortable" caring for our son.

I wondered how necessary that was. The NICU nurses had already taught me everything and told me I was more than capable. Even they felt Ryan should go home. "You know your baby better than anyone," they told me. "You can do this."

But if Dr. Kanton and Laura were both suggesting it, it must have been the right thing to do. Right? Why else would they recommend it if it wasn't the best thing for Ryan?

Maybe they mistook my fear for a lack of readiness. Of course I was afraid. Anyone in my shoes would have been. But they never asked me what I wanted or how confident I felt with my new skills. Instead, they asserted their authority in an intimidating manner, sending me right back to submission over self-confidence.

Sensing my hesitation, Dr. Kanton arranged for a representative from the children's hospital to meet Ryan and speak with me and John. We agreed to tour the facility and meet with their doctor to discuss her thoughts about Ryan's condition and her proposed plan of care. The coercion was successful, and on November 10, at ten weeks of age, Ryan was transferred to the children's hospital.

My days were no different over the next six weeks in terms of spending my time sitting at Ryan's side. He was now in an actual crib, which made my heart happy. It was a welcome dose of normalcy, and I could bathe him in a small plastic tub, feed him his bottles, read to him, and dress him in cute little outfits. I felt more like his mom than ever before.

Ryan was put on a busy schedule with bedside physical and

occupational therapy programs. He was getting stronger and making great progress developmentally. He was also growing, reaching seven pounds, which was a huge milestone.

Coming from the strict health and hygiene protocols of the NICU, the one glaring challenge was the lack of infection control among the staff. The simple, basic precaution of handwashing upon entering and when shifting from patient to patient was inconsistent. I'd have thought it would have been easy for me to say, "Please wash your hands," to the person about to touch my baby, but I didn't want to seem difficult. Instead, I posted a sign over Ryan's crib in big bold letters that read *Please wash your hands before touching me*. It wasn't as effective as I hoped.

Six long but productive weeks finally led to a scheduled discharge on December 23. I couldn't have asked for a better Christmas gift. I bought a ridiculous number of developmental toys, probably in excess of two dozen, that fostered tactile, visual, and auditory stimulation and stuck them under the Christmas tree, all beautifully wrapped. The home healthcare company delivered oxygen tanks, monitors, and respiratory equipment to our doorstep. We were ready, and a profound sense of elation filled my heart.

On December 22, one day before he was scheduled to come home, I was sitting by Ryan's side when a "Code Blue" shrilled over the loudspeaker indicating that a cardiac or respiratory emergency was taking place. I was distraught to see a commotion of doctors and nurses surrounding the crib next to us immediately following the vocal warning over the loudspeaker.

It took me a minute to process the emergency unfolding just feet away, but the severity became crystal clear as I observed the doctor inserting an endotracheal tube into the throat of the child with a now bluish-gray face. She grabbed an ambu bag, a self-inflating resuscitator, attached it to the tube, and pushed breaths into his lungs.

A tremor crawled up my spine. What had just happened? I turned away, wishing I could block it from my mind, struggling to concentrate solely on Ryan while saying a silent prayer for the child.

The next morning when I arrived to pick up Ryan, the room was eerily quiet. The crib next to Ryan's was empty. Had the child died? My body tensed with anxiety. I couldn't imagine how broken his parents must have been, especially with it being just two days before Christmas.

Selfishly, I forced my brain to focus solely on Ryan rather than on the events I'd witnessed the day before. I would pray for that family later. Now it was time for Ryan to come home for the first time, and I wanted and needed to celebrate this miracle.

I stood and watched Ryan sleep, torn between letting his small seven-pound body rest and wanting to wake him to get the process started so we could get the hell out of there. I chose the former and quietly placed his going-home outfit on the edge of his bed while stuffing all of his toys, photos, and clothing into a duffle bag. I wanted to leave no memory of Ryan behind.

When I was finished packing, I sat with my eyes closed, rocking back and forth and thinking of all that was ahead of us. Celebrating Ryan's first Christmas. New Year's Eve watching the ball drop at Times Square. Holding his hands out to feel his first snowfall. Giving him his first Easter basket. Imagining all the vacations we would take as a family.

Ryan stirred. I glanced at the clock on the wall. *Ticktock.*

Ticktock. Five minutes passed. *Be patient,* I told myself. We've already waited four months, let's do this on Ryan's time. Finally I stood, my hands on the side of the crib, willing him to wake up. As if feeling my gaze, Ryan let out a soft cry just before opening his eyes.

"Good morning, beautiful boy! You're going home today!" I picked him up, nestled him against my chest, and kissed his head. "How about I change your diaper, then feed you and get you ready to go?"

With Ryan cradled in my arms, I fed him his very last hospital bottle.

"Okay, now let's get that air out of your belly," I said as I shifted him to my shoulder, gently rubbing and patting his back.

John was absent that morning due to an important client meeting, so his sister, Jenny, came to assist and document the special occasion. With video camera in hand, she captured the final moments of our hospital life.

I kissed Ryan's cheek before I laid him down to dress him. He looked so handsome in his special blue-and-white knit outfit, wiggling around and cooing, seemingly proud as a peacock. I settled him into his car seat and covered him with a beautiful Christmas quilt.

Jenny had the video camera aimed at us. I lowered my ear to Ryan's mouth. "What's that, Ryan? Where's Daddy? I don't know." Turning to the video camera, I said, "Daddy, would you like to answer that?"

"Susan," Jenny cautioned, "remember you're on camera."

"Oh, I know," I laughed.

"That's why she said it," the nurse chided.

My laughter hid my loneliness. I hoisted the portable oxygen tank to my shoulder and set the car seat in the crook of my arm. As I thanked the staff and said goodbye, I felt immense gratitude to finally be done with hospitals. The taste of that long-awaited freedom was exceptionally sweet.

Jake greeted us as we entered the house. Unable to contain his excitement, his paws danced around, eager to smell this new creature. He sniffed at Ryan's feet.

"Hi, Jake, this is Ryan, your new best friend," I said, patting him on the head.

Jake followed us as I carried Ryan and the oxygen tank up the stairs to his nursery. I giggled as we entered the room because it was decorated with soft pink and green Laura Ashley floral wallpaper. When we'd purchased the house a year earlier, we decided to leave it the way it was in case we had a baby girl. I hadn't had the energy to redecorate it.

Holding Ryan at my shoulder, we did a 360-degree spin. "I will make this the perfect baby boy room for you, Ryan, with cars and trucks in all the colors of the rainbow. I love you so very much."

I held him just a bit tighter. We'd made it home.

Chapter Five

The scent of pine wafted through the room as I carried Ryan toward the tree on Christmas morning, the reflection of the white lights sparkling in his eyes. John had placed gifts for me under the tree, but I was holding my most precious gift in my arms. I swayed with Ryan to Mariah Carey's newest holiday hit, "All I Want for Christmas is You," singing each word specifically to my son.

"Well, now, that is a beautiful sight," John said as he came in with our morning tea.

I giggled. "Did you hear that, Ryan? Daddy said we're beautiful!" I kissed Ryan's head before setting him down into his baby seat next to his oxygen tank and monitor.

I never expected to have a baby attached to wires and tubes 24/7, but I didn't know any differently, so this was our "normal." One tall, green, heavy oxygen tank was stationed in Ryan's nursery and another in the family room. Whenever we moved Ryan to a different area, we disconnected his nasal canula from the main tank and reconnected it to a portable tank that I could carry on my shoulder like a backpack.

The level of oxygen support Ryan needed was determined by a probe wrapped around his toe with a long wire connected to a pulse oximeter machine. The probe had lights that detected the oxygen saturation level in Ryan's blood. That information was then sent to a digital display on the oximeter screen, letting us know how well his lungs were working. If the level fell below a certain preset number, an alarm sounded. But the probe on his toe was finicky and wouldn't work properly if Ryan wiggled his foot, preventing the machine from registering the oxygen saturation levels and causing frequent alarms.

Babies wiggle their toes a lot, so in those instances, I had to determine Ryan's lung function by observing him and checking for nasal flaring and chest retractions, which were signs of distress. If no signs were present, I would hold his foot still so the probe could send the signal to the machine to verify he was okay. I felt anxious the first few times the alarm sounded at home, but the pattern of false alarms quickly became evident.

I sat on the sofa as I sipped the sweet black tea, grateful for this moment, beholding the stacks of presents surrounding our son. "I think I overdid it," I laughed.

"You did, but it's okay," John said, tenderly squeezing my leg.

"I just want Ryan to have every possible advantage and opportunity. The occupational and physical therapists said that the sooner we begin early intervention, the greater Ryan's chance will be to reach his potential. Plus, it's Christmas, and if anyone deserves the world, it's him." I glanced down at Ryan, noticing he was fixated on the shimmering tree.

"It's hard to believe he's already four months old," John said.

"I know, and he's still so small," I replied wistfully. "But he'll grow over time and will be okay." I nodded, affirming my words as truth.

"Should we open presents?" John asked.

"Yes! I'll get one for Ryan." I jumped up off the sofa, my eyes bright with excitement.

John and I took turns opening Ryan's presents, showing them to him, and describing what they were for.

"Look, Ryan, this is a doggy with different colors and textures on the paws. Feel this soft yellow fur."

I took his hand, guiding it over the fur and down to each paw. Ryan watched as we opened gift after gift, ending with my favorite—and certain to be his favorite—Floppy Fellow, a small plush rattle toy made from every primary color with multiple textures and sounds. Ryan's eyes grew wide as I slowly moved his hand over the green terry cloth hat, sliding it down to the raised white polka dots sewn into the bright-blue velvet tummy that enclosed a squeaky sphere, and ending on the crunchy yellow kneepads.

I watched him in wonderment. "This is how it's supposed to be."

"Yes," John said. "After so many months, it's nice to all be under one roof. How about some breakfast?"

"Yes, please!" I had been so focused on Ryan that I didn't realize my stomach was growling.

While John cooked his specialty, scrambled eggs and toast, I fed Ryan a bottle and then put him down for a nap beside me in his bouncy seat so I could keep an eye on him.

Because of Ryan's lung disease, it was necessary to protect him as much as possible. That meant no Christmas church service and minimal visitors. Not attending mass was hard because

Christmas meant the world to us. Celebrating Jesus' birth aligned with celebrating Ryan, and since Ryan was our gift from God, we wanted to share him with our community. But his safety meant no church. We felt certain that Jesus would understand.

It turned into a perfect day of love, laughter, and gratitude with John's parents, his sister, and my sister Paula all doting over our little angel. Ryan was like the star on top of our tree. He bedazzled everyone with his sweet smile and beautiful spirit. He stared inquisitively into the eyes of everyone who held him as if seeking their love and acceptance. But he didn't have to. He already had it.

An abundance of joy filled our home as we witnessed the beauty of Christmas through our picture window, watching the snow blanket the lawn in white, as if Jesus was wrapping us in his robe. We went to sleep Christmas night feeling the blessing of God's grace and love.

We woke the next morning to Ryan's cry for a much-needed diaper change and bottle. I yawned but smiled as I scooped him into my arms and gave him what he needed. John offered to help, which I appreciated, but I declined his offer. I needed to hold Ryan in my arms as often as possible.

Those first few days of being home with my baby were the best of my life. Each morning when I opened my eyes, I experienced that split second of unawareness, followed immediately by the peaceful, joyful mindfulness of my baby being alive and at home. It was a welcome feeling to start the day with a smile. We got into a groove with naps, feedings, playtime, and bath time. From the moment he met Ryan, Jake adapted and was instinctively gentle. It was magical. We were happy.

Our deliriously blissful bubble burst two days after Christmas when Ryan's monitor began to alarm even though his foot was still. His oxygen saturation rate began to drop. I opened his onesie and saw his chest was retracting slightly.

"No, no, no. This can't be happening."

I increased the O2 flow by a half liter, nervously waiting for the double digits to rise. Once they were back up to ninety-eight percent, I exhaled loudly.

"You okay, Ryan?" I took his hand and sat next to him, praying for it all to just be a passing hiccup. Although he looked pale and seemed tired, he still smiled. "He must just be having an off day," I said to John, although I didn't really know yet what an off day was for a baby, especially for one on oxygen.

An hour later, the alarm sounded again—evidence that something was wrong. When I spoke to Ryan's pediatrician over the phone, he told us to take him to the emergency room.

John and I looked at each other, crestfallen.

"Hopefully, it's nothing serious. Let's go," I said as I switched Ryan's oxygen to the portable tank and wrapped him in my arms.

We were ushered right in upon arriving at the ER. There was no waiting, simply a "come this way" as we quickly entered a small room. This was the beginning of learning that a baby in respiratory distress took precedence over broken bones, lacerations, and sick adults.

Within seconds, a doctor strode in. "I'm Dr. Samuels. What's going on?"

Where to begin? I thought.

"This is Ryan." My voice shook. "He was born prematurely and has bronchopulmonary dysplasia. He was here in the NICU for ten weeks, then at a children's hospital for six. He just came home two days before Christmas, and now he seems to be having a harder time breathing."

"Let's take a listen."

Dr. Samuels moved his stethoscope around Ryan's back and chest. Ryan looked weaker and even paler than he had earlier that morning, and he seemed to be declining quickly.

"He's in respiratory distress and doesn't have much air movement in his lungs," the doctor said. "It's most likely a pneumonia. He needs to be admitted to the pediatric ICU."

"Wait, shouldn't he go back into the NICU?" I asked, my eyes widening as they swiftly moved Ryan out.

"No. Once a baby is discharged from the NICU, they don't go back. The next step is the pediatric ICU. This is the first of many more hospitalizations."

"What do you mean?" I asked with anguish in my voice.

"These babies with BPD have frequent illnesses and hospital stays. We'll be seeing a lot of each other."

"But the neonatologist never told us that!"

"They never do. They leave that to us."

My shoulders slumped as we hurried down the hall.

The PICU resembled the NICU in that it housed multiple beds in one room, but Ryan was now sharing this large room with children of all ages, including teenagers. Distressed over this new situation, I expressed my concern to the doctor. "Is it safe for Ryan to be with so many older kids? He's so tiny, and the others are so big."

"I promise you Ryan is in safe hands here and will be watched closely."

"Am I allowed to stay with him like in the NICU?"

"Yes, the same rules apply. You can stay all day, but not overnight."

The tests concluded that Ryan's rapid decline was caused by respiratory syncytial virus, RSV for short—the very same serious respiratory virus as the baby in the crib next to him a few days earlier at the children's hospital.

When I asked the doctor if Ryan could have caught it while he was there, he said, "Yes. The timing makes sense, and if no one else around him has been sick, that's the likely point of transmission, especially if the nurses and doctors weren't washing their hands in between caring for that child and Ryan."

I gathered myself and asked the question I feared most. "Is Ryan going to die from this?" My heart leaped into my throat as the words came out.

Dr. Samuels said, "We'll do everything we can for him."

"We just got him home!" I cried, grabbing the doctor's arm. "Please don't let him die!"

He looked into my face, and I knew he read the terror in my eyes. "It's obvious that no one prepared you fully for a BPD diagnosis. Let's first get your son through this, and then we can talk about a plan."

I felt comforted by Dr. Samuels. His words, and the confidence in his tone, suggested a prognosis of recovery. He remained attentive and communicative throughout, displaying an undeniable determination to help our child. He stayed close by those first few days, arriving early and staying late as Ryan lay lethargic and pale. I recognized his dedication and was grateful.

Sure enough, with the help of this new medical team, including Dr. Williams, a pediatric pulmonologist, Ryan recovered without requiring a ventilator. It was an astounding outcome.

Once again, our baby proved that his fragile eight-pound body didn't come near reflecting his internal strength and fighting spirit. After six days, on New Year's Day, Ryan came home for the second time.

With the start of a new year at hand, we tried to keep our enthusiasm high. But having the doctor tell us we should get used to being in hospitals still stung, so we remained cautious.

Through a contact of John's dad, we sent Ryan's medical records to a specialist at a hospital in Colorado, known as the leading respiratory hospital in the country, and scheduled a phone consultation. Surely the best pulmonologists in the country could create a better pathway for Ryan and for us.

"If we bring Ryan out to you, is there a possibility you could help him?" I asked.

Silence was my answer.

"From the stories we've heard," I continued, "you seem to work magic with lung diseases."

"Logistically, the flight and the change of altitude out here in Colorado would be too risky for Ryan," they told us. "Since BPD is a chronic condition for which there is no cure and only limited treatments, I'm afraid there's no additional care that we would be able to offer."

"Please," I said, "there must be something you can do for our son."

"I'm sorry. I wish there was."

We ended the call feeling desperate. "Now what?" I asked John. I knew he wanted to be able to give me an answer, but there was none.

The euphoria I had felt only a week earlier sank to hopeless dread. What would it mean if more hospitalizations occurred?

How much could Ryan take? How much could his damaged lungs take? How strong was he? I asked these questions to Dr. Williams during a follow-up appointment the following week and was left shaken by his response.

"There is no crystal ball. Only time will tell. There's not much more I can do. I think it's best for your pediatrician to be your point person going forward."

"But you're a pulmonologist, which is what Ryan needs. Shouldn't you be our point of contact?"

But he simply said, "The pediatrician will reach out to me if I'm needed."

Jolted by his cold statement, my mouth opened to speak but his eyes silenced me as if I was being dismissed.

I sat frozen for a moment before lifting the diaper bag and oxygen tank to my shoulder and cradling Ryan's car seat in the crook of my arm. "Thank you for your time."

I felt like Ryan and I were racing against the clock and the disease. He needed time to outgrow the BPD, but he wasn't gaining much weight. If he didn't get bigger, his lungs wouldn't get bigger. How could his lungs withstand more infections?

We had been under the impression that Ryan was coming home to stay for good, to recover and grow up, not to go in and out of hospitals. My hopes were being challenged, and I was questioning my ability to handle the road ahead.

By mid-January, Ryan had gained only one and a half pounds. His pediatrician diagnosed him with a "failure to thrive."

"What does that mean, exactly?" I asked, concerned.

"Your son is not growing at the rate he should be."

"But he's drinking bottles of my breast milk. Isn't that supposed to be enough? Should I be doing more?"

"Let's give him a bit more time. You're doing everything that you can."

I gazed at Ryan's precious face. His smile made my lips curve up slightly, yet I couldn't help but feel I was somehow failing him.

By the end of January, he had consistent tachycardia, meaning his heart was beating faster than it should have been, causing him to require more oxygen. I called the pediatrician, who instructed me to call Ryan's cardiologist. We made an appointment for that afternoon.

After examining Ryan, the cardiologist hung the ears of his stethoscope around his neck and said, "I don't know what's causing his symptoms. I suggest you go to the ER and have him admitted to the pediatric floor for tests." Noticing my eyes glistening, he handed me a tissue. "I know this is hard. I wish I could help."

"Me too," I said, brushing the tissue across my eyes. "Thank you." I covered Ryan's head with his tiny hat, kissed his forehead, and said, "C'mon, baby boy, let's go."

This would be hospital admission number three, and our first on the pediatric floor.

John was daunted to learn that we were back at the hospital. "How's he doing?"

"I don't know. I'm just so frustrated and it's breaking my heart to watch him struggle like this. Why can't he get better?" My voice trembled.

"I'm sorry I'm not there with you. I'll come by after work. Please keep me posted."

"I will." I set the phone back in the cradle and lowered the side of Ryan's hospital crib. I caressed his arms and legs while we waited for the doctors to arrive. "I promise you, I'm going to do whatever it takes to get you better and bring you back home."

Fear and sadness enveloped me as I wondered if I could keep that promise.

The difference between the PICU and the pediatric floor at that time was the level of care and supervision. In the ICU, patients were connected to monitors that communicated directly to the ICU team, and there was a nurse in the room 24/7. On the pediatric floor, the child was alone in the room, or with one roommate, with periodic visits from the nurse checking vital signs.

In Ryan's case, he was connected to a heart monitor and pulse oximeter within the room, but the signals and alarms didn't transmit to the nurses' station. As the parent of a baby in this situation, the vulnerability is inescapable. I worried not just for Ryan's health but for his overall safety as a defenseless baby. I stayed by his side as long and often as possible, sleeping in the chair next to him, leaving him only to use the bathroom and get a quick bite from the cafeteria.

Two days later, John and I sat together alongside Ryan's crib. Just as we were discussing how confusing and concerning this hospitalization was, Dr. Samuels, Dr. Williams, and Laura, the social worker from the NICU, walked in. They stood side-by-side before us almost ominously.

Dr. Samuels began. "After having a couple of days to observe Ryan, it appears that he may be aspirating during his bottle feeding due to reflux." The kindness emanating from his eyes was not lost on me.

"So that means that liquids are getting into his lungs, right?

Like when he was in the NICU?" I asked, my brows creased.

"Yes, that's what we believe."

I lowered my face into my hands.

"So, what now?" John asked.

"He needs a pH probe," Dr. Williams said.

I raised my head, looking from one doctor to the other. "What is that, and what does it do?"

"It's a test to determine whether anything is rising back up from his stomach and possibly getting into his lungs," Dr. Samuels said. "A small tube would be inserted into Ryan's nostril going down into his esophagus to record acid levels in his stomach over a twenty-four-hour period."

"That doesn't sound much different than him having a feeding tube in his nose," I said, "so let's do that."

"Well," Dr. Williams said, "we don't have the necessary equipment here to execute this test. He will need to go elsewhere."

Laura shifted on her feet nervously.

"Okay," I said, "so where do we go to have this done?" I was surprised a hospital of this caliber didn't have the equipment for what seemed like a simple procedure.

"We've reached out to a hospital in New York. They have a highly specialized pediatric respiratory department and they would like to try to help you," Dr. Williams said.

"New York? Isn't there somewhere locally we could have this done?" John asked.

I caught the doctors exchanging a glance before Dr. Samuels cleared his throat. "We think that Ryan could benefit from a 'tune-up,' so to speak. The head of pediatric pulmonology in New York is one of the best in the field, and we believe it's worth having her evaluate Ryan further, in addition to doing the test."

He just compared my baby to a car, I thought, *but okay, keep an open mind here.*

"So you're saying that taking Ryan there is not just to have the test done?" I asked. "You think that this doctor could offer other treatments to help him?"

"Yes, we believe that it's worth a try."

John and I looked at each other. Something didn't feel right but I couldn't put my finger on it. The specialist in Colorado had said he wouldn't be able to do much else to help Ryan, so why did these doctors think a New York doctor would be any different? On the other hand, we were only five months into this, and Ryan wasn't thriving. What did we have to lose by giving it a try?

We thanked the doctors and said we'd think it over and let them know by the next day. They left the room. Only Laura, the social worker, stayed behind. As I watched them go, I reflected on the fact that Dr. Samuels had been compassionate throughout the entire conversation, his eyes and tone expressing affection—contrary to the body language of Dr. Williams, whose curt responses reflected a cold and callous demeanor. His jittery feet had certainly made it seem like he couldn't wait to leave. What an odd dichotomy, I thought.

"How do you feel about all of this?" Laura asked us.

"I don't know," I said. "We want to do whatever is best for Ryan obviously, but this is all so new to us."

"Have you been sleeping here with Ryan?" she asked.

"Yes, I have. John's been going home to take care of our dog."

"You must be exhausted."

"I am. Not just due to lack of sleep but also the worry and fear consuming my mind. I just want to be a mom and a wife, and I feel like I can't be either. I can't sleep at home because I can't bear to leave Ryan alone on the pediatric floor, especially since there aren't any monitors connected to the nurses' station. What if something happens and no one realizes? He just seems so tiny and vulnerable."

"I doubt that would happen," she said, "but as a mom, I understand. I'll leave you two to talk. Please let me know if you need anything."

When she left, I turned to John. "Didn't you think that was a bit weird?"

"How so?"

"They each were so different in how they handled this. Dr. Samuels seemed to truly care, and Dr. Williams didn't. And why was Laura here? She's a social worker. The way they all came in together was just strange," I said, shaking my head.

I tried to put it out of my mind as we weighed the pros and cons of going into the city. We had no idea how many days we'd even be there.

Where would we stay? Could we handle the additional expenses? We would have to find someone to take care of Jake while we were gone. And there was the concern over how much a New York hospital would cost, and if health insurance would even cover it.

All were valid logistical issues. But as we watched Ryan nap, the one giant benefit took precedence over the short list of drawbacks: that medical care in New York could possibly help our baby. That was all that mattered.

My sister Paula was single and living in a one-bedroom apartment in the city at the time. When we called and told her about our conversation, she insisted we stay with her and use her bedroom.

"It'll be fun to have you guys here!"

"But we don't feel right taking your bed," I said.

Paula was adamant. "It's just for a few nights. I'll sleep on the sofa. Not a big deal. I would do anything to help you and Ryan."

"Are you sure?"

"Yes! I love Ryan as if he were my own. Whatever you guys need, it's yours."

We decided that New York City would be the next stop on our journey, and hopefully the last, given the high praise bestowed upon the specialist there. When I spoke to Dr. Samuels and asked who we should reach out to in New York to coordinate our arrival, his response perplexed me. "Laura is handling that and is coordinating transportation."

"I'm confused," I said. "We are planning to drive Ryan there ourselves."

"That's not how it works. We'll arrange for an ambulance to take him."

"Is that necessary? He's doing fine and is stable. Why do we need an ambulance?"

"Hospital protocol," was all he said.

I thought that it was a bit over the top, but who was I to question hospital protocol? Less than twenty-four hours later, I was in the back of an ambulance with Ryan and the EMS worker while John rode up front with the driver, battling the late-Friday-afternoon traffic between New Jersey and New York. It took two hours to drive just thirty-five miles.

When we arrived at the emergency room, I felt a sense of unease as the back doors of the ambulance opened. "We're here, Ryan," I said, clasping his little hand in mine and praying we were doing the right thing.

We were greeted by a hospital employee and followed behind the gurney as they guided us through the ER entrance. I was struck by the overall organization and professionalism, which brought me a small sense of relief.

Ryan's room was on the fourth floor with a large window overlooking the bustling street below. I was happy to learn it was a private room. We reset the crib with toys and photos and rested Ryan's music player on the nightstand. It had been a long, exhausting day, and Ryan's cry made it clear he was tired and hungry.

Just then, a new group of people entered the room. "Hi," one of them said, "I'm Dr. Lambert, the pediatric pulmonologist who will oversee your son's treatment while here. These are our medical students, who will be observing." Eight sets of eyes converged on us.

John and I nodded and said hello. "This is Ryan," I said and smiled.

"I want to listen to his lungs for a minute," Dr. Lambert said. "Could you put him up on your shoulder please?"

I did, and she moved her stethoscope over Ryan's back while the med students leaned in, eager to hear her findings.

"There seems to be good air movement throughout, which is encouraging," Dr. Lambert said. "We will keep him on a half-liter of oxygen for now. We'll schedule tests beginning on Monday to determine a treatment plan. The residents will be monitoring Ryan throughout the weekend and will contact me if needed."

"But today is only Friday," I said. "Why do we have to wait? Why can't we start the tests right away?"

"Because we have fewer lab technicians and diagnosticians over the weekend. Those that are here are focused on urgent and emergent care only."

"Then why we did come here today?"

"Dr. Williams made the arrangements for you to arrive today. Were you not aware?"

"No, we were not," John answered.

"Best to follow up with him. I'll see you Monday morning." Dr. Lambert smiled and left, the med students following in a line after her.

Ryan cuddled into my shoulder as I turned to John. "What the hell just happened? We could be at home for the weekend instead of sitting in yet another hospital dealing with more strangers!" A swell of rage rose in me. "Why would he tell us to come here on a Friday knowing that nothing would be done?! Why would he do that?"

The relief I'd felt less than an hour earlier was replaced with infuriation. The only thing keeping me from screaming was the fact I was holding Ryan.

Chapter Six

Awinter weekend in New York City can be magical: walking down Fifth Avenue alongside Central Park, beholding the snow swathing the trees and ground in white glitter, hearing the clip-clop of the horses' hooves on the street as they pull carriages carrying couples snuggling under wool plaid blankets, witnessing the joy on the faces of parents and children holding hands while gliding around the ice rink at Rockefeller Center, or sitting at a quaint table by the window at a sidewalk café savoring a cup of steaming hot chocolate. This was all at our easy disposal, but only if we left Ryan alone in his hospital room, which I would not do. Changing hospitals didn't alter the vulnerability factor, so I continued to bond with Ryan inside the four walls of our new space, relegated to enjoying the captivating energy of the city through the window.

It was Saturday and Paula was on her way across town to visit us. Having her close by while in an unfamiliar environment was comforting. Just a quick cab ride. Much better than a train or hours on the highways.

Ryan was on my lap while I read a picture book to him. Each

turn of the page presented an opportunity for him to feel differ-ent fabrics or surfaces—soft, scratchy, bumpy—and each turned his eyes into saucers of curiosity. Our immersion in the book was interrupted by the click-clack of heels coming down the hallway.

"Aunt Paula is here!" I stood excitedly, holding Ryan so he would see her when she entered. He squealed in delight the mo-ment she entered the room. I wrapped her in a warm embrace. "I'm so happy you're here!"

Paula tickled Ryan's tummy, reveling in his smile. "Where's John?" she asked me.

"He went to the office to catch up on some work. He's going to come back later, and we'll meet you at the apartment after Ryan falls asleep for the night."

"I actually have a date tonight," Paula said, blushing.

"Oh, exciting! Who's the guy?"

"Someone I met through a work colleague. Seems nice, but we'll see."

Paula was thirty-four, beautiful, kind, and smart. She had many dates and a few relationships, but none that had ever stuck. To say she was guarded was a massive understatement. Her walls were constructed of hundreds of bricks cemented to-gether, many feet high—thank you, Dad. As the oldest child, she'd experienced our parents' divorce and the subsequent abandonment by our father differently than I or my brother. She'd seen and heard things that shredded her concept of trust. Every now and then a brick would shift, leaving an opening for a man to inject the slightest bit of hope. She wanted to get mar-ried but was in no hurry, and she had no interest in settling. I knew it would take an extraordinary man to win my sister's heart, so I wasn't surprised when, that Sunday morning, she reported, "Another dud date." Rolling my eyes, I gave her a hug and left for the hospital.

The process began bright and early Monday morning. Fifty-five hours after our arrival at the hospital, Dr. Lambert stood before me. She was joined by a team of people clothed in blue scrubs, all peering at Ryan. "Good morning," she said. "From Ryan's chart, it appears he had no health concerns over the weekend."

"Yes, he seems to be doing well. Are we doing the pH probe today?" My voice lifted as I leaned forward.

"We'll be getting multiple tests ordered over the next few days—heart and head scans, specifically an echocardiogram to check on your son's atrial septal defect, EKGs for his heart and head, a brain ultrasound, and the pH probe."

A look of surprise crossed my face. "I thought we were here just for the pH probe. I didn't realize all that was needed." I just wanted to get it done and take him back home.

"The pH probe is necessary to see if Ryan is aspirating, but my goal is to improve his overall lung function, so it's important that we do all of these scans and tests to establish a baseline."

"Got it. Okay, that makes sense."

"Let's get started," Dr. Lambert said to the students. "This is Ryan, a six-month-old presenting with bronchopulmonary dysplasia due to his premature birth at thirty-three weeks' gestation, with a birth weight of only two pounds nine ounces caused by intrauterine growth retardation. He also has Down syndrome. Who can tell me the characteristics of Down syndrome?"

A petite female with a blond ponytail raised her hand.

"Almond-shaped eyes and low muscle tone," she said, smiling as if she knew she'd just gotten an A on the test.

"Yes, what else?"

"Some have heart defects," a young male with long curly dark hair confirmed with a nod.

As my sweet son just lay there, cooing softly, my insides were silently screaming. Why were they focusing on Down syndrome when the concern should be his lungs?

"Anything else?"

Blank stares all around, including my own. I was speechless from this line of questioning. I sat frozen, feeling like my son was being studied more than he was being cared for.

"Down syndrome is caused by an extra twenty-first chromosome during cell division, referred to as Trisomy 21," Dr. Lambert said. "Other characteristics include a large protruding tongue and short stature. Let's look at his palm. Do you see this line right here?" She turned Ryan's right hand over so all could see. Moving her finger along a line on his palm, she added, "This is called a simian crease. It's one of the most prominent signs of Down syndrome."

The students surrounded the crib, leaning in to see.

"Now let's listen to his lungs."

Although Ryan was calm, I was unprepared for each of the students to take turns moving their stethoscopes across his chest and back. I swiftly stood and placed both hands on the side rail of the crib. "Ryan's health is fragile. Is it necessary to have so many people touching him?"

"This is a teaching hospital, so the students will be observing Ryan as well as practicing on him."

If Dr. Lambert saw the look of concern on my face, she gave

no indication. I had not been told that this was a teaching hospital—one more piece of information that had been left out of the conversation, and one more experience for which I wasn't prepared. I didn't know what to do. Could I say no? Could I demand that they stop? This was my Ryan, a human being, not an object for practice. Feeling the need to comfort Ryan, I stroked his head until they left.

"Don't worry," I said, cuddling him against my shoulder. "This is just for a few days."

By midweek, we learned that the results of all tests and scans were "within normal limits." The pH probe that had been so pivotal showed minor signs of reflux, but nothing far above normal, ruling out aspirations during bottle feedings.

"If the bottle feedings are safe, why isn't he gaining weight?" I asked Dr. Lambert.

"I suspect that his effort to drink from the bottle is making his respiratory system work harder, thus burning more calories. I'd like to switch him to NG tube feedings to see if that helps."

I crossed my arms. While I was relieved to learn that Ryan wasn't aspirating, I was frustrated by the thought that he'd have to experience the invasive tube again. "I understand this is necessary to help Ryan, but I'm troubled that he has to suffer a tube again."

"Let's just see how he does, okay?"

I nodded.

One week later, Ryan's cheeks were filling out, his skin was creamy white and no longer mottled, and he displayed more energy when playing with his toys. Encouraged by these improvements, I asked Dr. Lambert if Ryan could be discharged soon.

"I still want to play with some of his medications and see if we can get him off the steroids," she said.

"How long do you think that will take?"

"Hard to say. Maybe a couple more weeks."

"Weeks?" I shuddered at the thought of another long-term hospital stay.

"Balancing out his medications is complex. Changes in doses require days of observation to ensure there are no negative side effects. We also need time to train you on inserting the NG tube."

"Do you mean that Ryan will be tube-fed at home and I'll be putting the tube into him?" My stomach twisted just thinking about having to do that to him.

"Yes. Given how significantly he's improved, tube feeding will be part of the ongoing treatment plan." This time, she must have seen the panic in my eyes, because she said, "Try not to be concerned. We see many babies with Down syndrome who require feeding tubes at home. The nurses will teach you everything you need to know. You can begin training tomorrow."

I placed my palms on my forehead. Carrying an oxygen tank and watching a monitor was one thing. Pushing a tube into Ryan's nose hoping it made its way successfully to his stomach was quite another. I trembled at the thought of harming him or causing him pain. How could this be expected of a mom?

Ryan began to coo as he shook Floppy Fellow and wiggled his feet in the air, his eyes shifting from the colorful toy to the bright-blue socks on his feet.

He had an astonishing way of talking to me without speaking, as if sensing that I needed to be brought back to the moment, to see beyond the feeding tube and into his entire spirit. He turned his head toward me and smiled, so pure and innocent, as if to say, "You got this, Mommy."

My lips curved upward, but my eyes were not smiling.

Sleep eluded me that night. My body was rigid with tension, my head unable to relax into the soft downy pillow. My brain was in a ferocious state of commotion, transforming thoughts of handling bendy feeding tubes into visions of slithering snakes. I hated snakes, and I hated what was now expected of me. Would I be able to snake a tube down into my child's body? Could any mother? *Should* any mother? I shuddered, desperate for slumber so I could shut off the terror in my head. Over the eight hours I spent in bed that night, I slept only a few, powerless to escape the formidable fear.

I walked zombie-like into Ryan's room the next morning, my hair falling in strings around my face, dark circles like black makeup under my eyes. Ryan was awake and being tended to by the nurse.

"Good morning," she said. "This would be a good time to teach you how to change Ryan's feeding tube. Are you ready?"

"Not really." I yawned.

She gave a sympathetic smile. "It's not as hard as you think. You'll see."

Unconvinced, I steadied myself as she began the tutorial.

"Feeding tubes should be changed once a month, so the first thing we'll do is remove the one he has." She gently lifted the tape on his face that held the tube in place. "It's best to pull the tube out quickly. It won't hurt him. Watch."

The tube was out in one swift motion. Ryan squirmed and whimpered, but he didn't seem to be in pain. I stroked his head.

The nurse gathered the supplies—the nasogastric tube, a five-millimeter syringe, disposable gloves, a marker, and tape.

We scrubbed our hands before putting on the gloves. Then she removed the tube from the sterile wrap.

"First, we measure how long the tube should be. We take this end and start by holding it at the tip of Ryan's nose, bringing it around to his ear lobe, and down to the midpoint between his breastbone and belly button. Then you mark it with a black line. Okay, now you do it." She handed me the tube.

Ryan stared at me as I repeated the steps.

"Good. Now that we have the appropriate length, we lubricate this end and insert it into the nostril. I'll show you first. You'll need to restrain Ryan's arms and hold his body still for me."

My eyes widened. "Restrain him?"

"Yes. If he moves, it's much harder to safely insert the tube."

I took a deep breath and did as she asked. Ryan wiggled, and I had to exert more force. "I'm sorry, Ryan. Mommy has to do this."

I blinked back tears seeing the confusion in his eyes, feeling him fighting against me, and hearing him cry out as she slowly inserted the tube, stopping when the black line was just outside of his nostril.

"Now we temporarily secure the tube by taping it to his nose like this, and then we check to be sure the tube is in his stomach and not his lungs."

Dear God, I thought. *No parent should have to do this.*

She attached the syringe to the tube and slowly pulled back on the syringe. Fluid flowed in. "The fluid will be either digested milk or gastric fluid. This is how we know the tube is in the stomach. If no fluid comes out, it means the tube is in his lungs, which can be fatal." She detached the syringe. "Now we switch roles." She removed the tape from Ryan's nose and swiftly pulled the tube out. He cried out, clearly agitated this time.

"He has to go through this again? Right now?" I picked him up, comforting him against my shoulder.

"Yes, we have to be certain that you can do this." She rubbed Ryan's back. "I know this doesn't seem fair, but it's necessary. I'll help you through this."

She took Ryan from me and laid him in the crib. My hands were shaking. "It's going to be okay," she said. "Take some breaths."

We rewashed our hands and put on new gloves. As I began to measure a new tube, Ryan grew anxious and fidgety. The nurse held him down while I marked the tube and lubricated the end.

"Just go slowly. Don't force it. If it feels like it's stuck, just pull it back out."

I did as she said, and the tube moved easily for me, but seeing my baby looking at me and crying directly under me because of something I was doing to him was agonizing. My tears fell onto his belly.

"I'm so sorry, Ryan. Mommy's so very sorry!" I cried as the black line reached the end of his nostril. The nurse taped the tube to Ryan's face and handed me the syringe, both of us relieved to witness the liquid flow in. "Thank God," I whispered.

"You did great," the nurse said, comforting me as she set up the feeding syringe. "Just hold him for a while as the formula goes in. It will be good for you both."

We rocked, and Ryan fell asleep in my arms. Yawning, I rested my head against the back of the chair. Sadness washed over me as I thought about what I'd just done. I would need help changing his tube at home, which meant John would have to be the one to hold him down. Would Ryan come to hate us both? I squeezed my eyes shut, yearning for the anguish to fade.

With Ryan's continued improvement, I was eager to get him back home. The recommended "tune-up" had already lasted thirteen days, and the upheaval in our lives was taking a toll on me. I was traumatized by the training, weary of being surrounded by sterile white walls and medical equipment, and exasperated by having to witness ongoing groups of medical students poking and prodding Ryan and studying his physical characteristics as if he were a strange creature. "He is a baby with Down syndrome, not an animal in a zoo!" I wanted to scream.

I had asked Dr. Lambert if we could finish Ryan's stay without the involvement of the med students, to which she replied, "If you refuse care from the medical students, then you and your son can leave my hospital."

Her words stung. I lowered my head in shame, feeling a burn inside of me. My role as Ryan's mother had once again been diminished to one of submission. I felt trapped, not just in the hospital but in my own body. My chest tightened as anxiety pulsed through my veins. I was desperate to get away from the doctors, the nurses, and the feeling of having no control over my life, no voice. I needed to be able to be in a place where I could make decisions, where my choices mattered, where I felt safe and free from prying eyes, from judgment.

The calm, composed concern I had displayed during the first week shifted to extreme irritability. I would sit with my eyes shut and my hands pressed against my head trying to squeeze out the tension, silently begging for our situation to change. I was locked in a spin cycle where impatience, self-pity, and guilt all reared their ugly heads. This was not lost on Ryan's nurses.

"Do you talk to someone?" a nurse asked me once.

"What do you mean?"

"Someone who can help you through this. What you're going through as a mom and as a family is very difficult."

"I talk to my friends and my sister," I said. "They help me."

"That's good, but sometimes we can't get the emotional help we need from those closest to us. You're in distress, and it may help to find a therapist or a psychologist who has experience dealing with trauma."

Her words cut through me like a blade against my skin. Tears blurred my vision as I looked at my baby, sleeping so peacefully, blissfully unaware of how sad and stressed I was.

"I see how deeply you love your son and how dedicated you are to his care," the nurse said. "You owe it to yourself to get the care you need. Just think about it." Her eyes were kind and hopeful as she handed me a tissue.

That evening, I broached the subject of a therapist with John.

"Do you really feel like you need one?" His tone of uncertainty was clear.

"The trauma of the last six months has worn me down. I've been doing my best to stay strong, but I'm falling apart inside," I said. I wrapped my arms around my stomach. "What I witness every day is wrecking me because I can't make Ryan better, and I just want him home. I want to go home." My voice choked with tears.

John took my hands. "If this is what you need, then of course. Just please make sure the therapist is in our insurance network." He pulled me close and held me until my sobs subsided.

With that, my mission to find help began. Someone we'd been introduced to through the Down syndrome community connected me to a female therapist near our home in New Jersey who had experienced similar trauma. This therapist came very highly recommended, and after a phone conversation with her, it was evident she understood and empathized. The only catch was that she wasn't an in-network doctor in our insurance plan, so the coverage was denied.

"But if this is the person who can best help me, why won't you cover it?" I asked.

"We can give you some names of other therapists that are in-network that you can try," came the response.

"Try? I don't have time to try. I need help now!" I was indignant. "My baby has been in hospitals for six months, and I'm losing my mind! I've already connected with this therapist, and she has personal experience with trauma. Please, I'm begging you to work something out for me. Please!" I felt heat infuse my face. "I'm on the verge of a breakdown. Is that what you want? Would you rather take a chance on something happening to me? Wouldn't those medical expenses cost far more than therapy?" I knew my behavior was irrational, but I was distraught. "Please help me," I cried.

Something I said must have penetrated because the representative on the other end of the line exhaled loudly and agreed to cover eight sessions.

"Oh, thank God. Thank you!" I sank into my chair, my labored breathing calmed by the knowledge that support would be available once we returned home.

Two days later, Paula suggested that John and I take the weekend off and enjoy the city. "It'll be good for you both. I'll stay with Ryan and watch over him so you have nothing to worry about."

"That's your only time off from work," I said. "Are you sure?"

"I'm sure. You've been by his side for two straight weeks. Besides, the hospital gray is starting to show on your face. You need some vitamin D."

I laughed with her. She was right. I needed fresh air and sunlight. But was I being selfish? I felt that I was, but over the past six months, the one consistent message given to me by the multitude of nurses caring for Ryan was, "You have to take care of yourself in order to take care of your son."

Even with that knowledge, the guilt of not being with Ryan resounded—but the risk of losing my sanity won out.

"Daddy and I are not going to be here for a couple of days," I said to Ryan as he rested on my bent legs, facing me with a smile shining in his brown eyes. "But Aunt Paula will stay with you, okay? Please know how much I love you, sweet boy." I held his small hands, my eyes begging him not to hate me.

"I know you don't want to leave him," Paula said, "but he'll be fine. Ryan and I are going to have fun! Aren't we, Ryan?" He giggled as she tickled his feet.

I lifted Ryan to my shoulder and breathed in the baby lotion scent on his skin and the sweet shampoo in his hair. I kissed every part of his face before handing him to John.

"Be good for Aunt Paula," John said. "Mommy and I love you very much."

"For God's sake, it's only two days. Go!" Paula said, gently taking Ryan from John.

"Thank you," I said and hugged her. I kissed Ryan's head and left with John.

It was cold outside, and even though I was shivering, never had the cold, biting winter air felt so good whipping across my face.

John pulled me close. "Are you hungry?"

"I'm starving! How about breakfast at Sarabeth's?"

"Sounds great." John hailed a cab, and off we went to begin our two-day respite.

When I quieted my mind, it felt like we were on vacation, but my heart knew better. The medical path we were on seemed to indicate that escapes would be few and far between, but knowing that Ryan's lungs would grow gave me hope that one day the three of us would vacation together—maybe building sandcastles on a beach or sledding down a snowy hill. The "where" didn't matter. Only the "when."

We were only ten hours into our day when thoughts of Ryan tugged on my heart, and I found myself yearning to hold him and kiss him goodnight. But as John and I cozied up to dinner, I focused on my love for my husband, my heart grateful for him, and for my sister who had my back and was keeping my sweet baby safe so that I could regain a semblance of strength and composure.

I collapsed into bed that night, my bones heavy from prolonged exhaustion. The serenity of the day fed my spirit and alleviated my angst, allowing my chest to calmly rise and fall. My last thought before drifting off was of Ryan in a peaceful slumber with God draping a protective blanket over him, and then over me.

The glow of the morning sun through the window roused me, and my eyes opened to a brilliant blue sky. I clasped my hands, stretched my arms over my head, and jerked my legs to untwist the sheet and blanket from my body.

Hearing the apartment door open, I lifted myself onto my elbows. "John, is that you?"

"Yes, it's me." He came through the bedroom door and handed me a bag with a blueberry muffin and a much-needed cup of hot tea.

I took a sip and he asked me what I wanted to do for the rest of the day. "How about we go for a walk, do a little shopping, then grab lunch? I'd like to go to FAO Schwartz to get something special for Ryan." He didn't need a new toy, but I needed to give him one from the best toy store in New York City.

People-watching in a city like New York is a guessing game. Who's happy? Who's stressed? Is someone celebrating or grieving? Why is that person yelling? What's really happening in their lives?

Faces don't always convey the truth. I knew that mine certainly didn't. Would anyone look at me and think that I'd nearly had a breakdown just a few days earlier? My smile hid that fact as I shopped for toys to bring to my chronically ill baby. I looked around, wondering if anyone else was faking it.

We lunched at a great restaurant on Central Park South. I devoured my burger and fries and rested my hands on my stomach as I sat back in the booth. "I know we told Paula we'd be back around five, but I feel rested and want to see Ryan. Would you mind if I go back to the hospital now?"

"Not at all," John said. "I have some work to catch up on, so I'll go to the office for a bit and meet you at the hospital around 5:30."

As I was whisked away in a taxi, I prayed I would be a better mom than I had been the week before.

I entered Ryan's room quietly, wanting to surprise him, putting my finger to my lips to shush Paula as she looked at me with raised eyebrows. She was holding him at her shoulder so he could gaze out the window. I tiptoed across the room and softly kissed the top of his head. He turned to see me, and a squeal of delight resounded throughout the room. Ryan's smile was always a constant ray of sunshine, but this time it radiated love.

"Hello, my beautiful boy!" I took Ryan from Paula's arms and held him close, kissing his cheeks, his forehead, his little hands. "Did you have a good weekend with Aunt Paula?" I knew he couldn't answer me, but the joy on his face confirmed that he had.

"Why are you back early?" Paula asked.

"I felt ready. The last thirty-six hours totally regenerated me and it was great to be away, but I missed him so much I wanted to come back."

"Where's John?"

"He went to the office to catch up on work. He'll be here by 5:30."

As Ryan took his afternoon nap, Paula and I sat cross-legged in the chairs by the window, chatting about the weekend. John showed up a few hours later, surprising us with cocktails. He pulled out two plastic glasses and a bottle of wine for me and Paula, and a beer for him.

"I'd rather have a beer if you have another," Paula said.

"Sorry, I only have mine," John replied.

She shrugged. "Okay, wine it is."

John made a toast. "To Paula. Thank you for giving us this

much-needed weekend break."

We laughed as we talked, feeling optimistic about the upcoming week. Then John pulled another beer from his coat pocket, opened it, and took a sip. Paula's eyes grew to large saucers. "I thought you didn't have another beer!"

Realizing that he'd been caught, John chuckled. "Oh, well, I only brought beer for me."

She rolled her eyes and shook her head. "I spent my weekend here with Ryan, and you didn't want to give me the extra beer?"

He lowered his head. "I'm sorry, you're right," he said, passing her the can. "Here."

"No, it's okay, just keep it." Paula let out an exasperated sigh before bursting into laughter. I put my head in my hands, thankful for her sense of humor.

The next week brought the closure we all so desperately needed. Ryan's discharge was scheduled for Friday, exactly three weeks after having arrived. His scarred lungs were functioning well on just an eighth of a liter of oxygen, the lowest amount needed since his BPD diagnosis, and his weight gain extricated him from the "failure to thrive" category.

While the hospital stay was stressful, Ryan's health had improved, so I was hopeful that these weeks would be his last away from home.

The light was back in my eyes as I walked into Ryan's room that Friday morning. "Are you ready to do this again, baby boy?"

I set his diaper and outfit on the mattress and kissed his head. The heat on my lips from my baby's skin was unmistakable.

"No, no, no," I moaned as I pressed my hand against his forehead.

Ryan was burning up.

"Please God, no, not again!"

The light in my eyes faded. Hope drifted out the door like an untethered raft.

Chapter Seven

I clutched the sides of the crib and held my breath as Dr. Lambert examined Ryan.

"He has a fever of 101, but air is moving freely through his lungs, so it's not a respiratory infection. Other than the fever, he seems fine," she said as she rested the stethoscope around her neck.

"Can we still bring him home today?" My eyes pleaded for the answer to be yes.

"I'm concerned, but it may just be a simple virus. Since his lungs are clear, I don't see any reason why not. Alternate Tylenol and Motrin every three hours for the fever and keep in contact with his doctor in New Jersey."

"We will." I exhaled in relief, my hands clasped together at my heart. Home was within reach.

I buckled Ryan into the car seat, grinning ear to ear at how cute he looked in his denim baseball cap, navy jacket, jeans, and tiny sneakers. His eyes seemed tired as he watched me.

"It's okay, Ryan, we're taking you home now," I said and squeezed his hand.

The excitement of going home changed each time. There was a hint of hesitancy, and nervous doubts still floated in my head. Would this homecoming stick? I wanted to believe it would, but the drifting thought of "what's next?" lingered. I was beginning to doubt my hopes. Was my subconscious trying to prepare me for more battles?

Someone told me, "Hope for the best but prepare for the worst." What was the worst in this situation? To me, it was that Ryan would never get better. There was no way in hell that I would ever allow myself to prepare for that. So instead, I focused on hope.

We were home only a few hours when Ryan's fever went up and he had explosive diarrhea. The pediatrician instructed us to bring Ryan to the ER, and he was admitted to the pediatric floor. The formula feedings were discontinued and replaced with IV feeds. Two days later, we were still waiting on the results of the stool cultures, but Ryan seemed better, so he was discharged.

Just as we were getting settled back in at home, his condition abruptly deteriorated and his fever spiked. We took him straight back to the ER. The stool cultures confirmed rotavirus, a GI virus, and clostridium difficile, bacteria that causes infection in the large intestine. It was also confirmed that Ryan had developed these infections at the New York hospital. His GI system was wrecked, and I was furious.

"How on earth could he catch both infections at the hospital?" My face and neck grew flushed as I demanded an answer from Dr. Samuels. "Another hospital made Ryan sick! How can this happen?"

It felt as if the room was closing in on us. My breathing became shallow as my fear for Ryan's well-being expanded with my rage. If he wasn't safe in a hospital, how could we ever keep him safe?

Dr. Samuels led me to a chair. "Sit for a minute."

Reluctantly, I complied, my fists clenched.

"Look," the doctor said, "Ryan's situation is a catch-22. He'll be in and out of hospital until he outgrows the BPD, but hospitals are breeding grounds for bacteria and infections, so the key is to get him better and get him out as quickly as possible. In this last case, and in the case at the children's hospital, Ryan was exposed to additional infections right before discharge. Not every caregiver, whether it be a doctor or nurse, complies with the handwashing and sanitation protocols, so things do get passed between patients. It shouldn't happen this way, but it does."

"That is crazy! Look at him!" I bolted from my seat. "Someone's carelessness put him in this condition! He's just a baby!" I yelled.

"I know, and we are going to do everything we can to get him better."

I stood at Ryan's crib, my arms crossed over my chest and my hands clutching my shoulders. His skin was so white, so drained of color, and his body was listless and depleted, just like mine.

For the next few days, Ryan was treated on the pediatric floor, with the pediatrician as our point of contact. Dr. Samuels, though, stayed involved in Ryan's care even though he wasn't an intensive care case. He seemed to befriend us, and we were thrilled to have an intensive care specialist so attentive to Ryan.

"Thank you for caring and being around so much," I said to him one afternoon.

"No need to thank me," he replied. "I'm happy to help in any way."

I glanced out the door into the hallway. "I'm surprised Dr. Williams hasn't stopped by. He must be very busy."

"Yes, he is, but…" Dr. Samuels began, then hesitated.

"But what?"

"That's not why Dr. Williams hasn't been in to see Ryan."

I looked at him quizzically. "What do you mean?"

He cleared his throat. "Dr. Williams doesn't want to take care of Ryan. He sees Ryan's case as too involved."

"Too involved? But he's the pulmonologist and Ryan has a lung disease. If he doesn't want to take care of Ryan, how will Ryan ever get better?"

"Dr. Williams wants a nine-to-five job, and with Ryan, emergencies will come at all hours of the day or night. He doesn't want that responsibility."

I lowered my head so he couldn't see the hurt in my eyes. How could a specialist not want to take care of a patient, a baby, my baby? What kind of doctor feels that way?

"I've gotten to know you and Ryan pretty well," Dr. Williams said, "so it may be best for me to be your point of contact once Ryan goes back home."

"Sure, I guess, if that's what's preferred," I stammered, feeling abandoned by Dr. Williams.

"And please call me Bob."

I was confused. Dr. Samuels had been the one to save Ryan when he'd had RSV right after Christmas, so he certainly was capable, But Ryan had a lung disease, which required a pulmonologist. Was I really hearing that the one pediatric pulmonologist in the hospital didn't want to care for my son?

As Ryan's hospital stay continued, Dr. Samuels—Bob, as we came to know him—in coordination with Laura, the social worker, recommended we consider having nurses assist us at home to help us adjust.

"We spoke with your health insurance company," Laura told me, "and given the ups and downs thus far, they're open to covering two eight-hour nursing shifts per day. You can determine what you want those hours to be, but I'd suggest having an overnight shift every night so that you can sleep. What do you think?"

I thought it was a great idea and didn't see why we shouldn't give it a try. As a private person, I didn't love the idea of having strangers in my home, but with John working long hours, I appreciated the opportunity to have someone with medical knowledge around, especially when Ryan's feeding tube needed to be changed.

Laura said she'd get the process started with the insurance company and contact the nursing agency on our behalf.

Ryan's hospital visit lasted ten days. Before we left, Bob gave us his beeper number and his home phone number. "If you need anything or have any questions or concerns, please reach out."

"Thank you," I said, and rested my hand on his arm, comforted by his dedication to our family.

When the nursing shifts began, Ryan was put on a regular schedule of physical, occupational, and speech therapies. He was now just over six months old, and this was the first extended period that we were able to focus on his development.

I worked alongside each therapist to learn the multi-faceted approaches and goals for each specialty, which allowed me to see my son through a different lens—one of living and thriving and not simply surviving.

"Ryan is very alert and curious," his occupational therapist told me. "That's a great combination, and a strong indication of how he will function as he grows."

"Really? That's amazing to hear!" I clung to her positivity and encouragement.

"Watch his fingers as he handles this toy. His grasp is strong, and you can see the intention in his eyes."

I watched Ryan's hands shake the toy, and I saw his eyes follow the toy's up-and-down movement. We had been told that Ryan's intellectual disability would not be known for years, but I was hopeful that he would have greater ability based on the inquisitive nature of his eyes. He looked at his surroundings with purpose, absorbing colors and shapes and faces, and he was intensely responsive to joy, discomfort, or pain, just like any other baby. Hearing the occupational therapist's optimism for Ryan's future validated my belief that he would flourish. He would need more help physically due to the amount of time he'd spent on his back in hospital beds, but that would come in time.

All signs pointed to a peaceful and joyous spring. March and April brought fields of rainbows with sprouting tulips and daffodils, and as Easter came, we celebrated with renewed faith that Ryan would prevail.

"Happy Easter, sweetheart!" I said, surprising Ryan with a plush stuffed bunny when he woke that morning. His eyes sparkled as he took it with both hands and studied it, cooing as he waved it back and forth before throwing it over the side of the crib. I chuckled as I picked it up and handed it back to him. We played that game repeatedly, my laughter growing with Ryan's smile each time the bunny reappeared.

Jake, like the incredible dog he'd always been, was a super star. As Ryan lay on his blanket in the family room, a tube attached from his nose and a wire from his toe, Jake would step softly around him, backtracking at times, instinctively understanding how sensitive of a field this was.

When Ryan reached for Jake, he'd gently sniff him up and down before licking his hand. I knew Jake would be an instrumental part of Ryan's cognitive and physical development. I envisioned Ryan playing fetch with Jake, and Jake loving and protecting Ryan. I had no doubt they were destined to be buddies.

Bob's check-in calls came once a week, and there was a sense that Ryan had turned a corner for the better. I enjoyed relaying the good news to Bob every time we spoke and it was comforting to hear from him, but in secret truth, I hoped to never have to see him or the hospital again.

One day, two months after Ryan's homecoming, the alarm sounded on his pulse oximeter as he slept. I figured the probe must have fallen off his toe, but when I went to check, I was stunned to find that it was still tightly on. His oxygen saturation rate had dropped to 93.

Ryan's breathing seemed okay, but I turned his oxygen up a bit to see what happened. I exhaled in relief as his oxygen saturation rate returned to 100. But the next day, it happened again. This time, I noticed Ryan seemed a little tired. Not wanting to take a chance, I called Bob. When I told him what was going on and asked him if we should bring Ryan to the ER, he said yes and that he'd meet us there.

As we loaded Ryan's portable tank, monitor, and bag of toys, I was hopeful this would only be a bump in the road and not a complete detour on our path to healing. Bob greeted us as we arrived through the ER doors. My gratitude for his presence was immense as I followed him into a room and laid Ryan on the bed. I held my breath as the nurse connected Ryan to the main oxygen supply and wired his body with electrodes.

Methodically, Bob moved the stethoscope around Ryan's chest and back. Ryan was quiet and still. Bob's eyelids tensed as he removed the stethoscope and let it rest on his collarbone. The nurse awaited his instructions.

"Set up a nebulizer with albuterol and corticosteroid and order a chest X-ray," Bob ordered.

She nodded, swiftly gathering the supplies. I held Ryan's hand as the nurse covered his face with the tube and mask supplying the medications.

Worry loomed loudly in my voice as I asked, "What's going on?"

"I hear crackles in his lungs, and the air isn't moving as freely as it should be," Bob said, sounding concerned. "The X-ray will tell us more. Try not to worry until we know what's going on, okay?"

He put his hand gently on my shoulder to comfort me. I nodded, my eyes locked on Ryan's face. The nurse put on a lead apron as the X-ray machine was wheeled in.

"This will just take a moment," she said. "Please step out." She opened the curtain for John and me to exit. Reluctantly, I released Ryan's hand.

The diagnosis was respiratory syncytial virus that led to a lung infection. Another bout of RSV, and another stint in the PICU.

"How could he catch RSV?" I asked Bob. "We've been so careful making sure the nurses and therapists aren't sick and that they wash their hands before touching him. And we don't take him anywhere other than the pediatrician's office."

Bob sat, leaning in toward me. "I have no doubt that you've been diligent in keeping him safe. If no one was sick, there's no way to know how he caught this. It could be as simple as an RSV germ on a piece of mail in your mailbox. The good news is he's been healthy for the last two months, so he's stronger now, which means we should be able to get him through this without intubating him. I'll consult with Dr. Williams on the treatment plan."

Day by day, with continuous nebulizer treatments and combinations of medicine, Ryan improved without a ventilator. Dr. Williams checked on Ryan each morning with an air of indifference, but Bob spent a significant amount of time each day with Ryan and me, chatting and laughing, seemingly trying to alleviate some of my anxiety. It was as if Ryan was his favorite patient. I loved that. After all, what mother doesn't want their child's doctor to provide special treatment?

John and I were both at Ryan's side on the fifth day when Bob came by. He and John shook hands, and John thanked him for his dedication to our son.

"Anytime," Bob said. "We all want the same outcome here. To get Ryan better and minimize hospital stays." He shuffled his feet nervously, then said, "How about I treat you both to lunch? There's a great place right up the road."

I told him I didn't want to leave Ryan's side and recommended he and John go, but Bob reminded me they had so few patients that the nurse could stay with Ryan the entire time. "You could use the fresh air and a good meal," Bob insisted.

I looked down at my sleeping child and hesitated before saying, "Okay, that sounds nice."

We were like old friends sitting in the booth enjoying delicious food and great conversation. How lucky we are to have such support, I thought, looking from John to Bob. John squeezed my knee under the table, relieved to see me relaxed.

After five more days, Ryan was scheduled for discharge on Mother's Day, my first with my sweet son. We arrived that morning to find Bob standing at Ryan's bedside.

I leaned in and kissed Ryan's head and said, "Good morning." As I did, I noticed he seemed tired. Something was off. "Is he okay?" I asked Bob.

Bob sighed like someone delivering bad news. "Late last night, Ryan had a few cyanotic episodes, likely caused by increased vagal tone."

"What does that mean?" I asked.

"Ryan may have been straining with a bowel movement, causing a vasovagal response that turned his face the color of an eggplant."

"Is that normal?" John asked.

"We haven't seen this before with Ryan," Bob said, "and it even scared me, but once we increased his oxygen, the episode ended, and his coloring returned."

"Should he be coming home today?" There was a note of panic in my voice.

"Yes, there's nothing we can do for this condition other than be ready with more oxygen when these episodes occur."

An hour later, while gathering Ryan's things, we witnessed one of these episodes. I trembled as Ryan's face turned blue. It lasted for just a few seconds, but it felt like an eternity as I begged God to make it stop.

"Turn the oxygen up like I just did," Bob instructed me, "and let the home nurses know to possibly expect this."

Over the past eight months, my purpose had been to bring Ryan home, to love him, to teach him, to protect him, and I had walked out of every hospital door with confidence. This was the first time I walked out of the hospital coated with fear.

Informing the night nurse about a potential cyanotic episode was quite different from personally experiencing one. At 2 a.m., John and I were awakened by screams for help coming from Ryan's nursery. We jumped out of bed and ran down the hall. Ryan's face was a bluish-gray, and the nurse was standing over him holding an ambu bag over his mouth and nose, squeezing breaths into him.

"C'mon, Ryan, take a deep breath," I pleaded.

The episode was over as quickly as it had begun, but the impact was lasting.

"This child should not be home!" the nurse said, shaking as much as we were. "I can't believe the doctor told you to handle this with extra oxygen."

My eyes were wet circles looking back at her because I had no idea what was right. Since Ryan's birth, I had learned to trust in the doctors, in their beliefs, in their orders. As a first-time mom, what the hell did I know? They had gone to medical school, so they knew best. Didn't they? I hadn't yet reached a point of implementing my mother's intuition, so I sat, feeling paralyzed, wondering if I should listen to the nurse or to Bob.

I called Bob early the next morning to tell him what had happened. "The nurse was terrified and said Ryan should be in the hospital."

"That is not necessary," Bob replied. "I assure you there is nothing we could do differently in the hospital. You are doing the right thing."

"Well, the nurses don't believe me. Would you fax me a letter explaining that so I can show it to them?"

"Yes, I'll do that right away."

When I showed Bob's letter to the day nurse, she shook her head. "I don't know if I'm comfortable with this." Her skepticism was understandable, so I called Bob and had the nurse speak to him directly.

The look on her face when she hung up was one of shock. Who was I supposed to trust—the doctor who knew Ryan best, or the nurses? I was desperate to believe Bob because of how deeply he cared, and I knew he would never put Ryan in harm's way. It also meant that Ryan could be at home.

As the nurses continued to question Bob's diagnosis and treatment plan—and in turn, me—I felt like a rag doll being passed between medical professionals. All I wanted was to be a mom.

Ryan remained stable all that day but had more frequent and longer-lasting episodes through the night. John left early for work, and as the sun rose, I left messages for Bob.

I circled Ryan's room waiting for the phone to ring. When I didn't hear back, I hesitantly called Dr. Williams and left a message with his answering service. I worried that he'd be angry at me for bothering him, especially so early, but I was frantic for guidance. I jumped at the ringing phone in my hand.

"This is Dr. Williams," came the curt voice.

After explaining everything that had happened, he told me to bring Ryan to the hospital.

"I'm confused," I said. "Bob told us to stay home and said not to bring him in, but I'm scared."

"You can either listen to me or not, but I believe Ryan should be seen," Dr. Williams said and hung up, apparently frustrated.

Unable to bear it any longer, I called the pediatrician and told him I would be bringing Ryan to the ER as soon as the day nurse arrived so she could help me. He told me he'd inform the hospital to expect us.

I rested Ryan on a blanket on the floor and lay by his side until the day nurse arrived. I told her what was going on and then went to get dressed. When I came back into the nursery a few minutes later, Ryan was blue, and the nurse was panicking.

"The ambu bag isn't working, and he's not breathing! Call 911!" she shouted.

I grabbed the phone. "My baby isn't breathing! Please send help!" I yelled. Then, to the nurse, I cried out, "Help him, please help him!!" Sobs choked me. "Breathe, Ryan! Breathe!"

I heard the sirens in the distance and sprinted down the stairs. As a police car came down the street, I opened the front door, frantically waving my arms for them to hurry. Two officers raced up the stairs behind me. Upon seeing Ryan lying lifeless, one swiftly tried to force oxygen into Ryan's lungs while the other radioed for the status of the ambulance.

"Please save him! Don't let him die!" I was on my knees, tears cascading down my face.

Less than a minute later, two EMTs bounded up the staircase.

The policeman moved aside to allow the paramedics in. "He wasn't breathing when I arrived," the officer told them, "but I was able to force air in, so he's stable for now."

"Okay, let's get him in the ambulance," one of the paramedics ordered.

I followed the stretcher down the driveway and jumped into the back of the ambulance with Ryan. I looked at my baby's colorless face as my body swayed robotically in rhythm with the ambulance as it sped around vehicles and through intersections. I could feel the wetness on my cheeks and could see my legs shaking, but I felt numb. I was frozen in shock and horror.

"Are you okay?" one of the paramedics asked me.

I shook my head and looked up at him with fear in my eyes. "This wasn't supposed to happen. Bob said he was okay," I mumbled. "Bob said not to bring him to the hospital." I choked out the words as wet drops landed on my legs. He handed me a tissue.

Fifteen minutes later, the ambulance lurched to a stop at the hospital and the driver ran around to open the doors. Bob and Dr. Williams were among the medical personnel waiting for us as Ryan was rushed into a trauma room.

"I can't believe his condition! Why didn't you bring him in sooner?" Bob demanded.

The heat rose to my face as a fire of anger enveloped my body. "Are you kidding me? Don't you dare lay the blame on me! I called you multiple times and you said *not* to bring him in. You even faxed a letter stating the same!"

He opened his mouth to speak but chose to remain silent.

The medical team surrounded Ryan. He was quickly intubated and sedated, and a multitude of lines were inserted into his fragile body, including a central line placed in his neck.

"Your son is in critical condition," Dr. Williams said, his tone cold. "He's lucky to be alive right now."

As I stood facing him, I clenched my fists so tightly that my fingernails broke the skin. "Bob told us Ryan was having vasovagal episodes and that there was nothing the hospital could do differently for him than what we would do at home. I did as I was told!"

"We can discuss this later," Bob interjected. "Right now, let's focus on saving Ryan's life."

Chapter Eight

Hours later, I stood at the end of Ryan's hospital bed, my eyes fixated on the tube in his mouth. "The nurses were right," I said. "He shouldn't have been home. Why did you tell me not to bring him in?"

Bob rubbed the top of his head and sighed. "I didn't realize how serious it was."

I moved alongside the bed and scanned Ryan's limp, ghost-white body. "He was blue on the floor, Bob. My child almost died right in front of me, and you 'didn't realize how serious it was'?" My voice cracked. "You were the last person to witness his condition before discharging him! The home nurses knew, so how did *you* not know? You told us there was nothing the hospital could do, and I trusted you!" The shrillness of my voice shattered the stillness in the room.

Bob simply lowered his head and said, "I was wrong."

The heartbreaking truth of his words stung. If he was wrong, then so was I. By deferring to Bob, I had denied our nurses' instincts and experiences, unwittingly putting Ryan in harm's way. But most unforgivably, I had taken Bob's words as gospel and allowed my unwavering faith in him to take priority over my maternal instincts. A part of me had been desperate to believe Bob was right so that Ryan could be home with me. It had been my first Mother's Day, and I'd been so determined to feel like a normal mom that my senses were darkened. I suppose I would have believed anything that would have supported Ryan being home. Was I a victim, or was I an accomplice?

"You have to save him, Bob. This can't be his last memory," I whispered.

Bob was present morning, noon, and night, determined to keep Ryan alive, but there was only so much a man and a machine could do. Much depended on Ryan's heart, lungs, and fighting spirit.

John asked the question I couldn't: "Do you think Ryan will be okay?"

To which Bob responded, "It's like we're on a raft in the middle of the ocean and there's no land in sight." I was shaken by that ominous statement, picturing Ryan tumbling off that raft into the dark abyss of the sea.

I held Ryan's hand tightly as I reflected on our last few months together, grateful to have had so many special moments and milestones. He had learned to bear weight on his arms while lying on his tummy, smiling brightly as he lifted his head and watched me cheer him on. He'd found the strength to roll side to side, flopping his toys back and forth, squealing when he underestimated his strength and landed face down on his belly, his big brown eyes wondering how he got there. My favorite moment of all had been feeling his hands move around my face, exploring my lips, my cheeks, my nose, and my eyes, with unmistakable curiosity and joy. He was growing, learning, and thriving. Now, once again, he was trying to survive.

I released his hand and sat with my elbows resting on the bed and my hands clasped around my mouth. "God, where are you? He needs you. *We* need you," I whispered. "You have the power to heal him and make all of this stop. Why aren't you making him better?"

My head fell into my hands as I wondered if God was even listening. In my mind, God could flip a switch and Ryan would wake up happy and healthy. Unless His plan was to make Ryan suffer, which would be crazy because the God I believed in wouldn't do this to a baby. So what the hell was the plan, then? What was the purpose? Was I being tested? Hadn't I proved my devotion to my very special child? Hadn't I been steadfast in loving him and fighting for him? Fine, God, give me a child with Down syndrome. I can take it. But why make him suffer so greatly?

My thoughts swirled like leaves in a gust of wind, up and down, flying around at different heights, uncertain of when and where they would land. The more I deliberated on the power of God, the more helpless and frustrated I felt, because if God wasn't healing Ryan, then how were mere mortals supposed to? Who were we fighting against—God, the universe, or ourselves?

Ryan was kept heavily sedated to keep him from fighting the ventilator. The moment there was even the slightest movement in his body, another dose of the paralytic was injected into his IV line. He looked like he was in a restful slumber, but the peaceful imagery was a mirage. At any given moment, Ryan could be awake but unable to open his eyes or move any part of his body.

That meant that the paralytic hid the reality of his suffering.

Selfishly, I was grateful for the emotional protection it offered me.

On the third day, it was proven that Bob had misdiagnosed the reason for Ryan's episodes. The culprit was bronchospasms, which cause the muscles that line the airway in the lungs to tighten, restricting airflow—a very serious condition treated with bronchodilators. This was confirmed because the spasms were occurring while Ryan was on the ventilator.

"I'm sorry," Bob said.

My eyes narrowed as I studied him. His eyes were genuine, but the words felt empty. This wasn't a misstep or a minor infraction. My child had almost died because of Bob's misdiagnosis, and there was still the very real possibility he might.

My stomach twisted at the reality that Ryan's lungs had been shutting down when he was at home and we'd been told there was nothing we could do. I stepped back, resisting the urge to slap Bob's face. Was "I'm sorry" the best he could do? How about "I was careless and reckless, and my mistake will haunt me forever" just like watching my son turn blue would haunt me forever. Did he think he deserved a pass just because he felt bad? What about what he had done to Ryan, to me, and to our nurses? I'd been devastated when Bob had blamed me when I brought Ryan to the ER. Now, finally, he admitted his almost fatal mistake.

"This is your fault!" I screamed, my face red with rage.

Bob cowered at my accusation, his eyes cast down in shame, and for a moment I pitied him. The storm of emotions I experienced over the next few days rocked me. Anger and fear held me captive. My beautiful little boy, with his contagious smile and spirit, had opened my heart to a world of possibility, and I knew I would not be able to live in that world without him. I spoke to God while wrapped in a veil of darkness. "If you take Ryan from me, you better be ready to take me, too." The certainty of my words shook me.

On the seventh day, the blackness gave way to a flicker of light when Bob was able to reduce the ventilator settings. "He's improving slightly, so we'll attempt to wean him from the ventilator over the next couple of days."

Hope was revived.

On the ninth day, Ryan was successfully extubated, breathing on his own with supplemental oxygen, but he remained in serious condition. His body was wrecked, leaving him unable to do anything but sleep. This illness caused more scarring in his lungs, so I couldn't help but wonder what effect this would have on his ability to outgrow his lung disease. Would it be hindered or, God forbid, halted? We had no answers to our growing mound of questions.

On day twelve, Bob approached me and John suggesting a team meeting to discuss Ryan's "future course." As Ryan's parents, we embraced this opportunity to gain perspective and develop a plan to get Ryan back on track. We met with Bob, Dr. Williams, the pediatrician, and our social worker, Laura.

Bob took the lead with Dr. Williams at his side. "Once Ryan is strong enough to leave the PICU, we want him to remain on the pediatric floor until he's deemed to be stable."

"When do you think that will be?" I asked.

"Maybe a few more weeks. He is still a very sick baby."

"How long do you think he'll need to stay on the pediatric floor?" John asked.

"It depends on his progress, but maybe about a month."

One month and two weeks after nearly dying, Ryan's condition improved enough to move him from critical care to a private room on the pediatric floor. Knowing that this was to be another extended stay, we decorated his room with his toys and pictures and set up his music player.

"All set, sweetheart!" I said and kissed the top of his head. "A few more weeks, and we'll be back home again."

The next morning, Dr. Williams surprised me with an early visit. He said he wanted to do a repeat pH probe on Ryan to confirm the absence of aspirations.

"Does this mean we have to go back to New York?" I asked and tensed, remembering the stress of that hospital stay.

"No, we have the equipment to do it here." The lack of emotion on his face matched the flatness of his tone.

I sighed in relief. "Okay, great. When can it be done?"

"I'll get it scheduled for one day this week." It was peculiar of Dr. Williams to suddenly take a role in Ryan's care. According to Bob, Dr. Williams hadn't wanted the responsibility for Ryan, so why the attention now?

Laura stopped by shortly after, offering support and lending an ear. "How do you feel about the plan?" she asked as I sat rocking Ryan.

"If a few more weeks here helps Ryan fully recover, then we're on board."

"This last hospitalization was pretty traumatic. Do you have any thoughts about everything that happened?"

"It was terrifying! Ryan almost died right in front of me. I don't know that I'll ever get his blue face and lips out of my head." My body shuddered and I held him closer.

"Do you think you should have brought him in sooner?"

"Definitely, but Bob kept telling me and the nurses not to. We were all upset and confused, but I trusted Bob, so the nurses trusted me."

"Do you still trust him?" she probed.

"I want to, but it hurt me when he tried to blame me for Ryan's condition and for not bringing him in sooner. It was his fault, not mine. He discharged Ryan when he shouldn't have." I took a breath. "Imagine a baby turning purple and telling the mom and nurses to just be ready with extra oxygen. Should I have known better? How could I? I'm not a doctor, he is! He was supposed to know better." Feeling my body tense, I stood and laid Ryan in the crib before continuing. "He finally had to admit to his mistake, but the damage was done, both physically and emotionally. Ryan's lungs are worse now and we don't know what that means for his future. Honestly, I don't know what to think or who to trust, but I do know that it wasn't my fault and I just want Ryan to get better so that we can go back home."

Laura's eyes displayed a hint of uncertainty. "Are you angry?"

"Why are you asking me all of these questions?"

"I want to help if I can."

"I appreciate that."

She looked at Ryan, then back at me. "Well, I'm around if you want to talk," she said and moved to the door. "I'll check in on you tomorrow."

I nodded. "Thanks. All that matters is that Ryan is alive and is recovering."

Two days later, I was reading to Ryan when Dr. Williams stopped by. I put the book down and shifted Ryan up to my shoulder.

"We've decided that Ryan should go back to New York for

the pH probe," he stated without a hello or even a glance at Ryan. His blunt lack of social graces left me shocked.

"Why New York if the test can be done here?"

"We would prefer it be done there."

"It's a simple test, so why send Ryan back to New York and uproot our family? If it can be done here, we want it done here," I said, determined.

He met my eyes with a flash of annoyance. "Very well."

Alone with Ryan, I couldn't help but wonder what had just happened. Why would Dr. Williams want to send us to New York? It didn't make sense and felt wrong. Maybe he simply didn't want to deal with us, as Bob had said.

The test was completed and concluded minimal aspirations as before, but with the additional damage to Ryan's lungs, the team developed a new strategy, which was introduced to us by the pediatrician. "We've discussed your son's course of treatment and are recommending stomach surgery to include a fundoplication and a gastrostomy tube."

"What are those?" I asked him, uncertain of the necessity.

"Since tube feedings are going to be a long-term requirement, we would replace the invasive nasogastric tube with a gastrostomy tube, which is a tube that would be inserted into Ryan's belly to provide nutrition directly into his stomach."

I moaned. "Will he ever be able to eat normally?" The thought of Ryan never being able to experience the taste of food felt cruel.

"Hard to tell. It depends on his growth and whether his lungs recover."

"And what is a fundoplication?"

"It's a surgical procedure where the top part of Ryan's

stomach would be folded over and sewn around the valve at the bottom of his esophagus to prevent aspirations of liquids into his lungs. It's the best way to protect his lungs at this point."

My head fell into my hands. How did we get here, I wondered. My beautiful, innocent child was already facing so many health and developmental struggles, and now this. Life was supposed to get easier for him, not harder. He was supposed to learn how to eat, not be tube-fed with a sewn-up stomach. He was supposed to learn to run and chase Jake around the yard, but he wouldn't be able to if his lungs didn't grow. Not to mention the heart defect that was still being monitored.

What would happen next? Would he be able to have any joys in life? Would he ever experience the taste and feel of melted ice cream or pizza sauce on his face like other children, or be able to eat popcorn while watching a movie?

"When would these procedures be done?" I asked with defeat in my voice.

"As soon as Ryan is strong enough. Maybe within a few weeks."

"If that's what you feel is best, I'll talk it over with John."

Ryan remained weak and slept a lot. Although his room was directly across from the nurses' station, I stayed by his side so that my face was his one constant. A cot was brought in so I could sleep there. I left only to get food and to shower.

John went to work and took care of Jake. As happens with chronically ill children, spouses have no choice but to divide and conquer, and we were no different. Ryan was too weak to restart any of his therapies, so we were limited to reading and cuddling, with Ryan often falling asleep in my arms.

While my world became even smaller, my resolve and

devotion to my child grew greater. For a few months, we'd had a taste of a beautiful life with our sweet boy, and I was determined to get back to that. If that meant sleeping in a hospital room away from my husband and home, then that's what I would do, even if it meant adjusting to being awakened throughout the night by the hallway light and noises each time the nurses entered the room to check Ryan's vitals. I didn't mind the visits. They gave me the opportunity to check on Ryan myself and to make sure he saw my face if he woke up.

After one week confined within the cold white walls of the pediatric floor, I longed to feel the warm summer sun on my face, so I carried Ryan to the window where the rays were streaming in.

"Do you feel that, Ryan? That's the sunshine." I closed my eyes, envisioning John and I picnicking on a blanket in the park, laughing, playing fetch with Jake, and blowing bubbles for Ryan to reach for. My peaceful moment was interrupted by an unexpected visit from Laura and the pediatrician.

"Mrs. Wilson, may we have a word?" Laura said.

I sat on the rocking chair and rested Ryan on my lap.

"The team has talked it over, and we think it's best for Ryan to go to a chronic care facility for long-term treatment before performing any more surgeries," she said.

"I'm sorry, what?" I was staggered.

"We would like to transfer him to the children's hospital that he went to after the NICU."

"Why?" I asked. "Just a few days ago, the plan was to do the surgeries and send Ryan home. Why the change?"

"We believe Ryan would benefit from long-term care in a different facility," the pediatrician said.

"Does Bob believe that?"

"Bob is not the doctor in charge, so his opinion doesn't matter."

"Is that why he hasn't been around?"

I caught the uneasy glance between them as neither answered.

"Well, I disagree," I responded adamantly. "Ryan should be home with us once he's ready, not in a facility. The answer is no."

The next day, they came again, this time pushing long-term care not as an option but as a decision.

"How can you want this for our child?" I snapped irately. "The children's hospital is where he first was infected with RSV! No, we want Ryan home."

"That is not an option," the pediatrician stated with feet firmly planted and arms crossed.

I recognized no sign of compassion or kindness in his eyes. Something terrible was happening, but I didn't know why. He had been Ryan's pediatrician for eight months, yet he was like a stranger to me.

John was incensed when I filled him in later that day. "What the hell are they trying to do? He's our son, not theirs!"

"I know," I said. "I'm scared. I think we should talk to a lawyer."

"Good idea. I'll get a name, and we'll reach out tomorrow." He held me before kissing Ryan and me good night.

I felt especially vulnerable that night in the hospital. Too consumed with worry to sleep, I paced in the darkness, shaken at the hostility I'd faced and distraught over the power they had demonstrated. They couldn't really force us to send our child somewhere against our will, could they? This couldn't possibly be legal, could it? Would they be doing this if Ryan didn't have Down syndrome?

There were too many questions to which I had no answers. I sat on the cot with my knees pulled to my chest, rocking forward and back, desperate for morning to bring the opportunity to gain clarity. Emotionally spent, I curled up under the thin hospital blanket, praying hard for strength and guidance.

Disheveled and exhausted, I groaned when they came again in the morning. "Have you given any thought to what we discussed?"

I chose my words carefully, unsure of how to respond. "John has had a busy week at work, so we'll talk it over this weekend." I nodded in an effort to appease them.

Later that day, I was able to consult with an attorney to see what our legal rights were. I learned that I would need to obtain a second opinion to either verify or negate the position of the medical team. Specifically, was it in Ryan's best interests to go to a chronic care facility? I hung up disheartened but determined to prove them wrong.

A woman with whom I'd taken a prenatal fitness class who also had a child with Down syndrome referred me to her pediatrician, Dr. Jones. He was affiliated with our hospital and knew all the players, and he expressed astonishment that this team was taking such a tough stand. He recommended we meet with a pulmonologist from another area hospital, Dr. Cooper. I gathered Ryan's medical records and made an appointment.

Upon review, Dr. Cooper felt he could help Ryan if we were able to transfer him to his hospital, Memorial Medical Center, for evaluation. The only obstacle was that since Ryan's case was so involved, he wanted one of Ryan's current doctors to remain involved, but none were affiliated with the new hospital. Even so, he communicated that there was still a chance he could provide care.

As Ryan recovered over the next several weeks, Laura persisted in questioning me like the caring social worker she was, so I shared my thoughts about the doctors, the stress in our lives and our marriage, and my fears for Ryan. She was one of the few people I could talk to, and I held nothing back—including my anger at what the team was attempting to force, especially since it was Bob's fault that Ryan had almost died. I told her that the more time passed, the more the tension between us and the team was escalating. She listened intently but offered no guidance. After she left, I wondered if I was naive to trust her discretion regarding my feelings.

A few days later, we learned that Laura had been assigned to gather information on "appropriate" facilities. Alongside Dr. Williams and Ryan's pediatrician, she enthusiastically surprised us with a presentation on a facility in Baltimore, Maryland—almost two hundred miles from our home.

"What do you know about this facility?" I asked.

"The doctor you spoke to in Colorado mentioned it to us. A pulmonologist he used to work with is now on staff in Baltimore," Dr. Williams said, apparently back in a speaking role.

"Have you ever been there or know of any child who has received care there?" I asked, looking intently at each of them.

"No," Laura said, "but it comes highly recommended. It seems to be the perfect solution."

"For whom? You? It certainly isn't the perfect solution for my child," I said. Sardonic laughter rose from my throat.

It felt like the hospital was turning against Ryan, against us. We felt like outsiders, like the accused, when all we had done was follow the doctor's orders. Had Bob's mistake become such a liability that they were willing to jeopardize my child's life just to get us out the door? If they wanted him out, why not discharge him home?

The second I asked myself that question, the answer hit me with tornadic force. They would never discharge Ryan. Because if they did and he died, they would have been the last ones to care for him and could be legally liable. They were protecting themselves from a possible future liability, and they wanted someone else to act as the middleman, a different facility to take legal responsibility. Their act of prioritizing liability over a life was abhorrent, and I was determined to not let them get away with it.

Another week passed before they called a meeting in a large hospital conference room. Paula came for support and as a notetaker. As she, John, and I entered, we were met with intense stares from a multitude of unknown staff members seated at banquet tables covered in white tablecloths and arranged in a giant square. The formality was foreboding, the antagonism petrifying.

Introductions revealed a hospital administrator, a bioethicist, the head of nursing, and a hospital attorney along with Laura, the pediatrician, Dr. Williams, and Bob, who we hadn't seen in over a month. Witnessing the imbalance of power, my insides spewed like a volcano about to erupt. Had I known, I would have brought our attorney.

The conversation began with the hospital administrator presenting a case review that entirely omitted the most crucial detail—Bob's misdiagnosis. Her goal to blame me was clear as she stated the hospital's intention to send our child to Baltimore.

"Given your son's near-death experience at home, we believe it is best he be sent to the facility in Baltimore where he can be watched more closely."

Like a mama bear protecting her cub, I responded with a roar. "*He* told us not to bring Ryan in," I shouted, pointing straight at Bob. "*He* misdiagnosed Ryan's condition. Don't you dare pretend otherwise!"

Until then, Bob, who had once been our friend and confidante, had remained silent and still, staring down at his hands. All heads turned when he stood and spoke. "My intentions were good, but I was complacent in Ryan's care."

My mouth was not the only one gaping open.

"See, he admits it!" I cried out.

"Sit down, Bob," the hospital attorney warned, like Bob was a defendant on the stand in a courtroom taking responsibility for the crime and getting reprimanded by his defense attorney.

"Regardless," the administrator affirmed, "your son's only chance is to go to Baltimore."

I pushed my chair back and stood. "Only chance for what? For living? Or for getting out of here?" My eyes were black with rage. "None of you have been to this facility of which you speak, yet you want our child to go live there. Would you send your *own* child there?"

No one answered.

"Will you agree to go tour it and meet with the doctor?" Laura asked.

"Do we have a choice?" I spat.

For purposes of due diligence, we agreed to meet the doctor

in Baltimore. It took a week and a half to get an appointment because the team there wanted time to review Ryan's records, yet our doctors were pressuring us in the meantime to confirm the move so they could plan the transfer. Their impatience was infuriating, their lack of humanity sickening. We stood our ground, telling them in no uncertain terms that we would never agree to send Ryan to a place we had not seen, nor would we put him in the care of doctors far away whom we hadn't even had a chance to meet.

When the time came, Paula stayed with Ryan while John and I traveled to Baltimore. Knowing she would be there to guard him lessened my anxiety, but as we drove down the highway and crossed into a different state, worry consumed me. I stared out the windshield, watching the passing cars and trucks spray rainwater into the swishing wipers, the dismal weather matching my mood. As we approached the facility, my breaths grew shallow. We were so far away from home, and all I could picture was Ryan feeling scared and forgotten, just like he would be if he was sent away.

We spent hours with the doctor and staff in Baltimore, and while they were very friendly and helpful, their plan for Ryan didn't offer any treatments that were different from what he was already receiving.

The tour was both eye-opening and soul-crushing. We saw children of all ages—toddlers, adolescents, and teens—with varying conditions including Down syndrome and other unidentifiable physical issues, strapped into chairs in the hallways staring into space, some drooling with no one wiping their mouths and chins, allowing the wetness to permeate their clothing. Where were their parents? All we saw were these lone children in the halls and staff behind counters. Was this where parents sent children they couldn't take care of anymore? Did they no longer even want to try? Was this where children came to die?

I felt my throat closing as I pictured Ryan in one of those chairs. I knew at that moment that my child did not belong there.

On the drive home, we talked by phone to Dr. Cooper and let him know we had decided to transfer Ryan to Memorial Medical Center under his care. He confirmed his support.

When we finally returned to Ryan, his smile was proof of the love we felt and the bond we shared. I held him close and promised I would keep him safe. He was in my arms for less than ten minutes before Laura knocked and entered, like a tiger pouncing, asking for our decision.

Needing time for guidance and a plan, I told her to give us a couple of days to think—to which she replied, "What is there to think about? Baltimore is the best option."

I held Ryan at my shoulder, rubbing his back. "This is my son's life we're talking about!" I hissed in disgust. "How dare you tell me what's best for him? You know nothing about our love or our bond. If you did, you'd support keeping Ryan with his family—with us."

"I believe I do know what's best for your family," she countered.

"Is that so?" I shot back, my words laced with hatred. "The stance you're taking is cruel and heartless. You're pitting an innocent baby and family against a hospital. You're a social worker. You're supposed to care! How can you live with yourself?"

Laura took a step backward, a look of shock in her eyes. The air was thick with silent aggression as she studied me. Ryan wiggled in my arms and turned to look at her. Her eyes shifted to his, and for a brief moment, I thought she recognized a human being rather than a pawn in their despicable game.

As soon as she left the room, I called Dr. Jones and updated him on what was going on. He sounded greatly concerned. "The position they're putting you in is crazy! I'm afraid of what they might try next."

"What do you mean?" I asked. "What else could they do?"

"I'm not sure, but their actions are excessive. Stand your ground and keep me posted."

Members of the team continued to hound me every day like participants in a rotating shift of torture duty. Our attorney advised me not to engage with any of them, especially Laura, and told me not to answer questions under any circumstance.

Frustrated by my silence, the tension deepened. Three days later, John and I, as a united front, told Laura and Dr. Brady that we wouldn't agree to send Ryan to Baltimore and instead wanted to transfer him to Memorial Medical Center under the care of Dr. Jones and Dr. Cooper. Laura's jaw dropped, and the pediatrician's face turned red. John put his arm around me as we stood firm in front of Ryan's crib, daring them to challenge us.

The following morning, a multitude of footsteps closed in on Ryan's room, alerting us to an onslaught by the team, the hospital attorney, and the administrator.

Dr. Williams took the floor as they surrounded us. "You have two options. Either take Ryan to Baltimore or Memorial. If you don't do one of those, we've been advised by our legal counsel to seek guardianship of your son."

While those words cut deep, our attorney had warned us this might happen. Nevertheless, we were disgusted by the mere mention of guardianship. But because the other option laid before us was a transfer to Memorial, we were okay with it. Or so we thought.

Not ten minutes after the group left the room, the pediatrician called to tell me that Dr. Cooper was no longer willing to take Ryan in at Memorial Medical Center. "That leaves you with Baltimore or a court battle," he said.

My hand trembled with such intensity that the phone fell to the floor, followed by my body. With my faith in humanity depleted, I crumbled into a ball. How could they take away our sweet, beautiful little boy? On what grounds? We had done nothing wrong and yet we were being bullied to give up our son. I begged God to wake me from this nightmare.

I took a deep breath, willed my body to stand, and called Dr. Jones. When I told him what I'd been told, he was stunned. "The fact that they would stoop to such a low level is outrageous. You have to get Ryan out of there. Sit tight, I'm going to make another call."

Within the hour, I received a call from another local pulmonologist at a third area hospital. His name was Dr. Abrams. He told me that he'd just spoken to Dr. Jones and said, "I'm happy to take over Ryan's care and will arrange for a transfer today."

Unable to compose myself, I sobbed into the phone.

Dr. Abrams' voice was strong and comforting. "It sounds like this has been a horrendous experience for you and your family, especially for your son," he said. "In all my years practicing medicine, I have never and would never institutionalize a child with Down syndrome, BPD or not, and it's crazy for anyone to suggest it."

"I don't know how to thank you," I said, my voice choking. "You're saving our lives."

He told me he would contact Dr. Williams and call back with information on the timing of the transfer. As we waited nervously, unsure of how Dr. Williams would react, we received another call. This one was from Dr. Cooper.

"Mrs. Wilson," Dr. Cooper said, "I'm calling to be sure you understand my position and the situation."

I was confused. "What do you mean?"

"After you told your doctors that you wanted Ryan transferred to my care, they called to inform me that they'd be suing for guardianship and that my hospital would be in the middle of the fight. I couldn't take on your son's case under such conditions, so I had to pull out. I hope you understand."

I felt like I'd been sucker punched. I couldn't take a breath. "My God," I gasped, my lips trembling. "They intentionally sabotaged our plan. How could they undermine us in such a ruthless and heartless way?"

"I'm sorry," he said. "I truly wish I could help."

Ten minutes later, Dr. Abrams called to tell us the transfer team was thirty minutes out. John went to get Ryan's car seat, and we hurriedly packed everything, leaving no trace of our hostage situation.

As we were putting the last of Ryan's belongings into the bag, a man wearing a white polo shirt and cargo pants knocked on the door. "Mrs. Wilson?"

"Yes," I said hesitantly, unsure of the stranger entering the room.

"Dr. Abrams sent us to transfer your son."

Relief flowed over me as I lifted Ryan from the crib. "Time to go, Ryan." As I buckled him into his seat, he reached up to touch my cheek.

With no time to waste, Ryan's seat was secured onto a stretcher, and we were led down the hall, onto the elevator, and out the front door of the hospital. We moved quickly, my eyes darting around and my head turning every few seconds in a near panic, expecting at any moment to be chased down by hospital security. As I sheltered in the back of the ambulance with Ryan and John, my eyes remained focused out the rear window waiting for police cars to appear for a chase, as if I was an escapee from prison.

Chapter Nine

There are three types of traumas: acute, which results from a single incident; chronic, which is repetitive and prolonged; and complex, which involves exposure to varied and multiple traumatic events. Ryan and I had been through all three—his traumatic birth, being held hostage in a hospital, and experiencing the multitude of crises and near-death experiences since his birth. This last nightmare paralyzed me with terror.

I was still looking over my shoulder when we arrived at Averton Hospital, half expecting to be ambushed by the gang that had so ruthlessly betrayed us at Ryan's previous hospital.

All rationality was lost. I was on edge, reliving the emotional torture of the past two months, feeling alone and overwhelmed, unable to process the scene before me. My brain was traumatized and I was in survival mode.

As the stretcher holding Ryan was carried from the ambulance, I stayed at his side, holding his hand and hovering over him like a shield.

Ryan yawned and let out a soft cry.

"We'll be settled soon, sweetie," I told him, hoping I wasn't lying.

Once through the doors of the ER, my eyes quickly scanned the surroundings, searching for any sign of the enemy. My throat tightened when a man approached.

"The doctors are waiting for you on the pediatric floor," he said as he guided us. "This way."

Hold it together, I thought. *Don't fall apart.*

Another hallway, another elevator. A set of double doors. Then a row of faces staring at us. I swallowed hard as they approached.

"Hello, Mrs. Wilson, I'm Dr. Abrams."

"And I'm Dr. Landon. I'll be your son's gastroenterologist."

"Hi," my voice shook. "This is Ryan." I desperately needed them to see him, to look into his eyes and feel his spirit, his potential, his love.

"Hello, Ryan," Dr. Abrams said. He smiled at Ryan and spoke sweetly. "Aren't you a cutie!" He ruffled Ryan's hair, and Ryan smiled back.

The doctors were gentle and kind as I presented Ryan's history, fully aware of the nervousness in my voice stemming from my shocked state.

"It's okay," Dr. Abrams assured me. "Take your time."

I had just ended my dissertation when we were joined by a woman with a sweet smile and short blond hair. She introduced herself as Dr. Richardson, Dr. Jones' partner.

"I'm so sorry," she told me, "Dr. Jones is still at the office and can't be here to greet you. But I'm so happy to be meeting you and Ryan!"

With those words, my composure shattered and I broke

down, unable to hide my anguish. If not for Dr. Jones' initiative and assistance, our family would have been torn apart and Ryan would have been exiled to Baltimore. The depth of gratitude I felt toward him, his partner, and everyone there flooded from me.

"They were going to take my baby away from me," I cried, tears tumbling down my face. "Are they going to come here to take him?"

"No, no, they're not," Dr. Richardson said. "You're safe here." She pulled me to her and held me until the sobs subsided. "Clearly, you've been put through hell, but you're both safe here. I promise you, Ryan is safe with us." When she handed me a box of tissues, I saw her eyes were wet.

"They can't do anything to you now that he's here," Dr. Abrams reiterated.

I dried my face with a tissue. "You're absolutely sure they can't take my baby?"

"Positive," Dr. Richards confirmed.

"Tomorrow, we'll meet and develop a plan to get Ryan back home with you," Dr. Abrams said confidently and reassuringly.

"Will we get Ryan back home?" I asked.

"That's the plan," he smiled.

As I unpacked Ryan's things, I contemplated the frightening power a medical institution can have over parents and a child. How many other families had been affected by doctors and hospitals trying to conceal their actions? How many families had been broken up, unable to find the strength or the resources with which to fight and protect their children? How many other parents and children had been terrorized? I shuddered at how the complicity of a hospital administration would so callously attempt to destroy a child's life to protect the hospital's bottom line, accreditation, and reputation.

As nighttime fell, I lay on a cot listening to Ryan's breathing, calmed by his peaceful slumber. For the first night in months, I was able to get a good night's sleep, believing the nightmare to be over.

Over the next few days, I was encouraged by the demeanor of the hospital staff and the newfound support for our family. The doctors shared our goal of having Ryan live at home and not in hospitals. After days of evaluations, it was determined that Dr. Jones would maintain a significant role in Ryan's care, but Dr. Abrams would be his primary care physician since Ryan had a respiratory disease—finally, a logical medical decision. Both doctors examined Ryan daily, showing crucial attention and care.

"Ryan's condition is much more stable than I was led to believe by Dr. Williams," Dr. Abrams shared with me.

"I'm not surprised," I said. "Ryan should never have been held in the hospital for months. It was cruel."

"Let's get the abdominal surgeries scheduled and go from there. You'll probably be here for a few more weeks, but you will get home."

"We will get home," I repeated. A smile moved across my face. Hope! Dr. Abrams smiled back.

The gastrostomy and fundoplication took place a week later. These were Ryan's first surgeries, and I was scared. In the best of circumstances, surgeries come with risks. With Ryan's lungs and heart compromised, the risks were tenfold. When the nurse came to take Ryan, I couldn't let go of his hand. What if he died on the table? Would this be the last chance I'd have to touch him, to kiss him, to love him?

"We will take very good care of your son," the nurse comforted me.

I kissed my baby's forehead. "I love you so much, Ryan."

"Time to go," the nurse said as she released the lock on the wheels of the bed.

As they pulled away, my grasp on Ryan's hand was gone.

*   *   *

I sat in the cafeteria booth watching the steam rise from the paper cup as the tea bag steeped, anxiously waiting for the time to pass. A young couple sat nearby, sharing a muffin, happily chatting. An older woman sipped a cup of coffee and read a newspaper. Who were these people, I wondered. Were their children in surgery too, or were they just visiting loved ones?

I contemplated their purpose as I sat sipping my tea, fiddling with sugar packets, making color-coded stacks. Weary, I opened the book I'd brought but closed it when I realized I was reading the same paragraph over and over again.

The ticking of the clock on the wall alerted me to the need for a change of scenery. I found my way to the hospital chapel, grateful to have the room to myself. I knelt below the crucifix and took a deep breath.

"God, please watch over Ryan. Please be with him and with the doctors who are working on him. Guide their hands as they do what needs to be done. I know you can make him better, so please do that, God, please."

I stood, lit a candle, then settled myself on a chair in the back. As I studied the artwork on the wall, the chapel door creaked open, giving light to the dim shadows. I considered the woman who entered, her head down, a tissue in hand, lines etched on her face. She knelt at the altar in silence, her shoulders rounded forward. I could feel her pain.

Knowing that she would want privacy, I said a silent prayer for her and left. After roaming aimlessly through the hallways, I found myself outside of the PICU just in time to get an update from a man in blue scrubs.

"The surgery is going well and Ryan is doing fine," he told me. "They should be done soon. Why don't you wait in his room so you're there when he's brought back?" He swung the door open, allowing me to enter.

A pretty nurse with flawless ivory skin and dark hair approached. "Hi, I'm Maria. I'll be Ryan's nurse today." She smiled warmly and pulled a stool over. "You can sit here while you wait."

"Okay, thanks."

This PICU was more intimate than the last, consisting of three rooms, each with two beds. There was a calmness to it, and it felt safer, less intrusive than what we'd experienced before.

I heard someone say my name and turned. His eyes were kind. "I'm Dr. Darby," he said, "the pediatric intensivist. I'll be monitoring your son in the PICU after surgery. He should be here soon."

I said hello and wondered if they were all really this nice or just handling me with kid gloves. A bit tentative, I sat rigidly on the stool, my hands folded in my lap. I wondered if they knew what had happened and why we were here. I had to imagine that everyone knew since it was part of Ryan's history. Did Dr.

Darby know Bob or Dr. Williams? If so, what did he think of them? God forbid they were friends. I just hoped they could all keep an open mind while getting to know us and make informed decisions based on their own interpersonal experiences with us.

My thoughts were interrupted by the double doors opening and wheels squeaking through. I jumped off the stool as Ryan was brought in. The feeding tube was no longer in his nose, but he was intubated. Upon seeing the fear in my eyes, Dr. Darby said, "The tube is temporary. As soon as the sedation wears off, we can extubate him."

I sighed, overwhelmed with relief.

Next, the surgeon stepped forward. "The procedures went very well," he said. "We'll keep him in the PICU for a few days as he recovers."

Impulsively, I wrapped my arms around the surgeon, catching him off guard. "Thank you so much!" I said.

"Just doing my job," he replied.

A week and a half later, after learning how to reinsert the stomach tube if it happened to fall out, I brought Ryan home. It had been almost three months since he'd seen his nursery. But we were back, and we had enormous trust and support from our new medical and in-home nursing teams.

Ryan's first birthday was just around the corner. "What should we do to celebrate your birthday, Ryan?" I asked him, his eyes rounded like saucers. "I know! Let's get lots of balloons and a really big cake!" I gleefully kissed him all over his head and face, leaving him giggling.

The weather on his birthday was sublime, just like it had been the day he was born. How far we had come in one year! I was so proud of my son, and so impressed with his spirit and inner strength. Although still small, only fourteen pounds, he was growing and thriving, and breathing well with minimal additional oxygen.

"You're a magical little boy, Ryan," I told him.

I was in awe of him. He inspired me more than any person ever had. On a daily basis, he taught me how to believe, to trust, to live with humility and gratitude. Ryan was the most flawless combination of innocence and grace. He was the most imperfectly perfect gift I had ever been given, and now was my turn to give him an imperfectly perfect birthday celebration.

Since we still needed to protect his health, the birthday party was limited to a few family members gathered outside on the deck, with no other children. Big balloons with trucks, cars, and Sesame Street characters, all in bright primary colors, covered the perimeter, dancing around in the breeze as if Elmo, Cookie Monster, and Big Bird were all waving to each other. Mounds of presents were placed on the table adjacent to a server holding a rectangle cake decorated with Elmo's face and the words *Happy 1st Birthday, Ryan!* He clapped his hands when he saw his favorite red face on the white background. Of course, Ryan couldn't eat the cake, but that didn't mean he didn't deserve one.

We were a family, doing family things, albeit limited to very small gatherings. Every week, I took Ryan to see Dr. Abrams. These were simple outings, but they became my favorite days because I got to bring Ryan out in public, proudly wheeling him in his stroller for all to see. I didn't care that the looks people gave me were looks of pity. How could I expect them to understand my joy as they looked at a baby with Down syndrome, a nasal canula in his nose, and an oxygen tank strapped over my shoulder? I wanted to say to them, "Isn't he beautiful?" but never could get up the courage.

In-home therapies were back on track, and for the first time, a lollipop was introduced during Ryan's session with Julie, his speech therapist.

"While Ryan receives his nutrition through the feeding tube, it's important to expose him to various tastes and textures orally to open up his taste buds and stimulate his lips and mouth," Julie explained. "With lollipops, especially, he'll learn how to close his mouth and his lips around the taste."

Julie lightly pressed the lollipop against Ryan's lips, prompting his mouth to open. The second the lollipop touched his tongue, he smiled, bopping his head side to side.

"That's good, Ryan," Julie said. "You like that one? Let's try something else." She removed the lollipop and replaced it with a textured bumpy finger cover dipped in lemon juice. The moment the juice touched his tongue, Ryan's eyes squeezed shut and his face squinched up. It felt cruel to laugh, but we couldn't help it.

"That's what sour tastes like, RyRy," I chuckled.

Taste testing became an important daily activity. We experimented with lollipops in every color of the rainbow. Julie used a kit of tips with various purposes like a brush tip for gentle gum massage and a bite-and-chew tip for Ryan to feel what it would be like to chew.

Ryan was also progressing with his physical and occupational therapies. He was unable to sit or stand, so to get a toy, he had to roll from side to side, stretching his arm as far as he could until he was finally able to reach it. His therapist called that "problem-solving."

With the end of summer came the burnt-orange hues of fall.

Scarecrows stood guard over fields of pumpkins as families picked apples from the orchards. It was my favorite season, and I wanted to share it with Ryan.

I carried him outside and set him and the oxygen tank next to me in his bouncy seat with Floppy Fellow. I held up an orange mum. "See this, Ryan? This is the color orange." I repeated this with the red, purple, and yellow mums before planting them in our front gardens. Every now and then, Floppy Fellow would go flying and I'd fetch it, returning it to Ryan by walking it up his legs, over his belly, and resting it on his head. I giggled each time he looked at me wondering where Floppy Fellow went.

On a glorious Indian summer Saturday, John, Paula, and I swooped Ryan up and spent an afternoon at a country farm, picnicking under a secluded tree drinking apple cider and eating pumpkin doughnuts. Dressed in brown corduroy overalls, a cream long-sleeve Henley shirt, and a red plaid baseball cap, Ryan looked like a Baby Gap model. I thought he was the cutest baby there despite the many "Oh, how sad" looks sent our way. Ryan's eyes gleamed, and his face radiated happiness. It was the perfect day.

One week later, Ryan's oxygen requirements increased—our signal to bring Ryan back to the ER and to notify Dr. Abrams to meet us there. My feet felt heavy walking back through those doors. Each time we brought Ryan home, I clung to the prospect of permanence. Would this one last? Each time he went back to the hospital, my fear replaced hope. Would this be it? Would Ryan make it through?

Ryan had a mild respiratory virus, which landed him in the PICU for three days. Two weeks back at home were followed by another short stint in the PICU in November. Unlike at the prior hospital, a bond formed between Ryan and his nurses. These were female nurses of all ages, some with full-grown children, some with young children, others married with no children, and a few single with no plans to have children. All were from different walks of life, but all with one commonality: they loved Ryan, so I loved them.

They engaged with him, always approaching him with a smile, speaking to him as if he could understand, and taking the time to know him through me. They asked about his developmental progress at home. They wanted to know what his favorite toys were, what cartoons made him light up, and what music made him clap his hands. To them, Ryan was a developing baby with special needs, a child deserving of love and support and not an inconvenience or a liability. For a parent of a chronically ill special needs child, that type of human understanding is an extraordinary gift.

While his recent illnesses were mild cases resulting in brief hospitalizations, Ryan continued to grow weaker. After the severe ups and downs of his first year, I was distressingly mindful of the tragic long-term consequences every respiratory illness could have. Winter was just beginning, and I fretted about what germs might be lurking on our mail, on packages, and on anything that was brought into the house. Would we be able to keep Ryan safe?

My fears were realized in December when Ryan was diagnosed with the flu, unable to breathe, and back in the hospital on a ventilator. It was this illness that had me waving a white flag to the universe. Since Ryan's birth, I had fought like hell against doctors and the health care system, exhaustively doing everything in my power to ensure Ryan's survival, his quality of life, his safety, and my sanity. Seeing him back on a ventilator, I felt like I had to bow to fate and end the fight-or-flight response to which I'd become so accustomed. The facts were clear: There were no miracles coming our way, and his disease wasn't going away any time soon. We were in this for the long haul. I would need to accept that trauma would be a part of our lives for many more years while clinging to the belief that one day, Ryan would be okay and his life would be amazing.

I vacantly stared out the window watching the snow swirl from the sky. Maybe we would have a white Christmas, I thought, yearning for Ryan to make it home to see it.

"How are you holding up?" Dr. Darby asked when he came in to check the ventilator settings.

"Honestly, I'm scared." I shook my head in frustration. "This is the fifth time in fifteen months that he's been on a ventilator. How much more can his lungs take? How much more can he take?"

"He's a strong little boy. I think he'll pull through this."

I nodded, wanting the words to ring true. During his short fifteen months of life, Ryan had only been home for a total of four months, all for varying periods. The absence of continuity was taxing. Not only was it stunting Ryan's developmental growth but also our ability to thrive as a family.

Because of the multitudes of IVs put into his small body since birth, and because of the certainty that his condition wasn't going to improve anytime soon, the doctors recommended inserting a portable catheter into his chest, which would provide a fast and easy way to give Ryan IV fluids and medications, especially under emergent situations.

"Is that really necessary?" I asked Dr. Darby when the chest catheter was first mentioned.

He said he thought it would be the best course of action for Ryan. "As it stands now," Dr. Darby said, "his veins are so small and hard to access, especially after the hundreds of IVs he's already had. We wouldn't have to constantly stick a needle in him to find a vein, so it limits his pain and protects his veins."

When I asked if it would be a safe procedure, he told me it was a very simple surgery. He said the port would be placed under Ryan's skin and attached to a catheter that would be threaded into a large vein above the right side of his heart. We would be able to use it to draw blood and administer medications and fluids.

Since saving us from captivity, it was clear that these doctors had one goal: to protect Ryan and our family. Knowing this allowed me to trust in Dr. Darby's belief that the port-a-cath would be beneficial. Half-heartedly, I gave my permission.

The surgery was seamless, and after a few days, the ventilator settings were slowly reduced as Ryan began taking intermittent breaths on his own—our precious child proving his astonishing strength once again. On the fifth day, Dr. Darby successfully removed the endotracheal tube, and Ryan was breathing independently.

"Hi, Ryan, Mommy's here," I said as I caressed his head. His eyes were heavy, but they saw me. "You're going to be okay, I promise."

Dr. Darby moved his stethoscope around Ryan's chest. "His lungs sound much better," he said. Then he smiled down at Ryan. "You really are quite the warrior, little man."

Ryan let out a whimper and closed his eyes. I stroked his cheek with my fingers. "Rest, sweetie. I'll be here when you wake up." I wrung my hands over my head, releasing the tension in my shoulders.

"He has a remarkable fighting spirit. I've never seen anything like it," Dr. Darby said.

I looked around at the sterile room. "I was wondering," I said. "Since it's almost Christmas, can I get a small tree for him to have here?"

The doctor said yes, as long as it was artificial and small enough to fit on a small table, so after getting the all-clear to run out while Ryan slept, I grabbed my coat and bag and left. The stones crackled under the tires of my car as I turned into the parking lot at Hall's Garden Center, fortuitously finding a spot right at the front door. Fresh greenery and berries lined the shelves, followed by row after row of vibrant red poinsettias. Christmas music played over the speakers and I smiled hearing Mariah Carey's voice, remembering swaying with Ryan the year before in front of our tree. I strolled through the shop looking for the perfect small tree when an older gentleman approached.

"Can I help you find something?" he asked.

"I'm just looking for a small fake tree," I told him.

"What kind of space is it for?"

I wavered, unsure of how much to disclose, but his eyes were so kind that I told him. "My baby is in the hospital in the ICU, so I wanted to give him a Christmas tree. It has to be small enough to fit on a tabletop."

He looked around and went over to the prettiest tree. It was covered in white lights and red bows. "This one."

"How much is it?" I asked.

"It's our gift to you and your baby."

"No, I couldn't possibly take it," I said.

"I insist. I'm Mr. Hall, the owner. Take it. I want your child to have a magical Christmas."

"Are you sure?" I asked, and he nodded. I thanked him profusely and embraced him, hoping he could feel my gratitude for the gift he'd bestowed upon not only Ryan but also me.

Ryan was still sleeping when I brought the tree in. Nurse Maria was sitting at a table by his side. "That's a pretty tree!" she exclaimed.

"It is, isn't it? It has lights! Is it okay if I put it on top of this side table and plug it in?"

"Yes, he'll love seeing it when he wakes up!"

From that simple moment grew a bond that would become unbreakable. Ryan was the only patient in the PICU during the Christmas holiday, so the staff made it all about him. Volunteers from different groups and organizations showered Ryan with gifts. They had been instructed to hand the toys to me so that I could disinfect everything, and then I put them under his tree to open on Christmas Day. Even Santa came to visit, and Ryan and I teamed up to sit on his lap together. Ryan was captivated by Santa's white furry face, and when he tried to pull on it, Santa let out a loud, "HO HO HO!" Ryan's eyes opened wide as he looked from Santa to me.

Chuckling, I said, "That's Santa's sound, Ryan. He goes 'HO HO HO.'" I cuddled him into my chest. The love I felt in that moment for this incredible little soul sitting on my lap was like a fierce, Heaven-sent force.

Waking on Christmas morning, I hurriedly dressed and ran down the stairs like a child running to the tree to open presents—only instead of doing that, I dashed to the car to get to the hospital to see my baby and to wish him a Merry Christmas.

When I saw Ryan dressed in a green and red outfit with Santa on the front, I knew the nurses had done that for us. Then I looked up at a long piece of art paper hanging on the wall over his crib. My hands went to my mouth as I looked at Emily, one of Ryan's other nurses.

"Did you do this?"

"Yes," she told me, "and Ryan helped."

The sign had Ryan's hand and footprints in bright red and green paint. It read *Merry Christmas, Mommy and Daddy! Love, Ryan.*

I had no words. Even now, it overwhelms me to think of it.

Later that morning, we got ready for all of the family to come celebrate Christmas with us in the hospital. I carefully picked Ryan's Christmas outfit: a red turtleneck and khaki pants with suspenders. He was quite dapper!

Paula arrived carrying an armful of gifts. While John stood on the opposite side of the bed with a video camera in hand, Ryan sat on my lap in the rocking chair, patiently waiting for his plethora of presents. Paula's hand became like an extra appendage as she helped him open the first box. Out came a bright blue-and-yellow accordion.

"This is amazing! It's perfect for him!" I placed Ryan's hands underneath mine on the handles and gently pulled and pushed while the sounds filled the room.

Turning to John, Paula asked, "Is the video camera on?"

I laughed. "I know what you're going to do!"

Paula took the accordion, squeezed it firmly back and forth, and recited, "I must, I must, I must increase my bust."

Ryan was startled by the volume of laughter in the room.

"Do you remember that?" Paula asked me.

"Oh yeah, I remember," I said, giggling.

As young girls, we'd been led to believe that if we squeezed something back and forth like that, it would make our breasts bigger. *Wrong.*

More family members arrived and many toys were opened, including a colorful toy phone with a dial sound and ring tone. John put the phone to his ear and said, "Hello? Oh, yes, you want to speak with Ryan?" He put the phone in Ryan's hand. "It's for you."

Ryan looked at him quizzically.

The pretend phone call was interrupted by a knock on the door. It was Dr. Darby. "Merry Christmas!" he said, joining us. Then, turning to Ryan, he said, "Oh, don't you look handsome!"

I smiled at him warmly. "Merry Christmas! We have something for you."

John handed Dr. Darby the card and gift we'd prepared for him. He opened the card, taking time to read my heartfelt message, his appreciation clear from the way he looked at me.

"Open the box," I urged excitedly.

Dr. Darby unwrapped the tissue paper to find a framed collage of photos of Ryan with hospital staff, including one very special picture of Dr. Darby holding Ryan just a week earlier.

"Hey, RyRy, look, it's us!" he said and turned the frame to show Ryan. "This is really amazing, thank you. We're putting this up on the wall." He bent down to kiss my cheek and then ruffled Ryan's hair. "Dr. Abrams will be in around 7:00 p.m., but I'll be around if needed. Is it okay if I leave this here so the staff can see it?" he asked, holding up the collage.

"Of course," I said. "Merry Christmas!"

After he left, Paula asked me what my card to Dr. Darby had

said. I handed it to her, and she read it out loud.

"To the entire PICU team. When we first brought Ryan to Averton, we were filled with apprehension and fear because we didn't know what to expect. In a very short time, you turned that fear into comfort and confidence. We are grateful for your tireless efforts, constant support, and the obvious love you have for Ryan. Thank you all for being so special."

Paula pressed the card against her heart, and her eyes grew misty.

"Oh, no," I joked, "are you going to cry?"

"Maybe!" she joked back.

The joy of Christmas and the love in the room that day sparked an undeniable energy fostering the belief that Ryan would continue to conquer his illnesses. I could feel God's presence and knew that He would not leave Ryan's side.

Ryan was discharged home just a few days later. With the new year approaching, I fixed my gaze firmly forward in hope. That hope was realized in the most unexpected way when we learned that I was pregnant with my second child.

Ryan was going to be a big brother.

Chapter Ten

When Ryan was just weeks old in the NICU, my OB/GYN said to me, "As soon as your body is recovered from the C-section, you should get back on the horse and have another baby right away."

I cringed at the thought of having sex, of my body hastily being cut open again. My thigh muscles tightened as I reflexively squeezed my legs together. As a grieving and frightened new mom, I couldn't comprehend the idea of opening myself up again physically and emotionally.

Did he think having another baby would erase the trauma? Was another baby supposed to replace Ryan if he died, or was that same baby supposed to take my mind off having a sick child with Down syndrome? Maybe my doctor was searching for a solution to assuage his guilt for missing the signs of Ryan's intrauterine growth retardation. Or maybe he was just a guy trying to "fix a problem." Whatever his thought process was, he didn't know what was best for me, but God did. God waited to give us this second miracle. And this was God's timing.

My bare feet sank into the plush carpet as I stood over the

crib listening to Ryan breathe as he slept. "Hey, sweetheart, you're going to be a big brother," I whispered, gently stroking his cheek with my fingers, contemplating the multitude of possible outcomes. Ryan could have a sibling to play with, to laugh with, to love and to be loved by, to learn from and to teach. Or he might never get to know his sibling. What if this baby was born prematurely? What if this baby had Down syndrome too, or a different syndrome or disease? Or, God forbid, what if Ryan died? What if this baby died?

Feeling my heart begin to race, I squeezed my eyes shut and shook my head from side to side, desperately trying to control the overwhelming panic created by the runaway train my brain had become.

Stop! You can't think like this! I silently ordered myself. Having only experienced this single trauma, it never occurred to me to ask myself, *What if this baby is born full-term and healthy?*

I wanted to believe that God would send us a healthy child, but I knew that nothing was certain, and I feared I would not be able to handle more sorrow.

Ryan was still drained from the flu, so our days back at home were quiet. No therapies, no visitors, no outings. Sesame Street and Barney became our entertainment. Ryan loved the sounds and colors and would clap along, bobbing his head back and forth. I was grateful for those vivid stuffed characters because they transported us to a world of kindness and love, a world without tubes... or fear.

Just two weeks later, the pulse oximeter alarmed, indicating the need for more oxygen.

I was always on guard when the alarm sounded, ready to grab Ryan's baby bag and get him to the hospital. I studied his chest and his nostrils. Neither suggested respiratory distress.

"You okay, RyRy?" I lifted him from the crib, resting him against my chest. He seemed tired but was breathing fine.

Three days later, the alarm coincided with nasal flaring and chest retractions, so there was no mistaking our next steps. I took Ryan back to the ER and within hours, he was back on a ventilator being treated for bilateral pneumonia—an infection in both lungs.

Everyone was stumped. How? Why? Would his lungs be strong enough to endure yet another infection so soon after the last? I wasn't the only person afraid of the answer to that question. Concern and distress were etched into the faces of the doctors and nurses as they worked to keep Ryan stable.

Since this infection had come on so quickly, the doctors performed a bronchoscopy, an endoscopic procedure that allowed visualization of the airways and lungs to see if maybe there was something in his lungs that an X-ray wasn't picking up, like a tumor, cancer, or an obstruction.

I was relieved that the results stated *typical conditions of bronchopulmonary dysplasia*, but I was also exasperated because the BPD was only getting worse and causing a consistent decline in Ryan's lung function. We would come to learn it was also stressing his little heart. During this PICU stay, Ryan's blood pressure was consistently high, another condition added to the already long list of medical concerns. It was followed by a new diagnosis of biventricular hypertrophy secondary to pulmonary hypertension—an increase in the muscle mass of both of Ryan's ventricles due to pressure overload caused by his lung disease.

"No, this can't be," I said in denial. "His little body can't handle that. Are you really telling me that my baby now has heart disease on top of lung disease?" I looked from Dr. Darby to Dr. Abrams, my eyes begging them to tell me it wasn't true.

Their facial muscles tightened, their concern as obvious as mine. Two of my baby's major organs were at risk of failing. Two. How many small babies are able to survive that?

"Ryan has proven over and over again how strong he is," Dr. Abrams said. "I've never seen a baby fight so hard to survive so many critical illnesses. His spirit is extraordinary. Don't lose faith." He put his hand on my shoulder and I clutched it as desperately as I clung to his words.

After five days of tears and prayers, Ryan was successfully extubated. Against all odds, he came back to us again. I was certain that once he was able to speak, the words "I give up" would not be a part of his vocabulary.

Now that Ryan was recovering, I shared our happy news with the hospital nurses.

"I'm pregnant," I announced, the corners of my mouth lifted.

"Congratulations! That's great news!" Maria exclaimed as she gave me a long hug.

"That's amazing! What a gift you're giving to Ryan!" another nurse, Tara, said before ruffling Ryan's hair. "Ryan, you're going to be a big brother!"

Although still exhausted, Ryan smiled.

"How far along are you?" Maria asked.

"Just eight weeks, so we aren't telling many people yet. But I wanted you both to know."

"How are you feeling?" Tara asked.

"I'm exhausted and my boobs are killing me, but otherwise, I'm fine," I giggled. It felt good to laugh and to share such happy news with these nurses who so clearly loved my little boy. "I need a new OB/GYN. I don't want to stay with the team that delivered Ryan. I don't trust them. They should have caught the fact that Ryan stopped growing at twenty-eight weeks. Can you recommend anybody?"

"Yes," Maria said confidently, "I have the perfect doctor for you. He's attentive and caring. You will love him."

Two weeks later, we were back home again and I began my new prenatal care with Dr. Hanson. Maria was right. He was warm, kind, compassionate…and handsome. I would come to learn that many of the young moms in town had a crush on him, not just because he was cute but because his bedside manner was what every exhausted, emotional, and irrational pregnant woman needed. He provided support and understanding, taking time to talk to each expectant mom as if they were the only person he knew who was having a baby, no matter how large the crowd in the waiting room grew. He seemed to know exactly how we were feeling, and he made sure we knew we weren't crazy to be blubbering over nothing.

As we approached the twelve-week pregnancy mark, my belly grew to a small mound and I allowed myself to be just a bit more excited for the future and less anxious about a miscarriage.

"Ryan, would you like to have a brother or a sister?" I asked, sitting beside him while his liquid dinner flowed from the feeding machine tube down into his tummy.

"Ba ba ba ba ba," he babbled in response, squirming under the soft buckle that held him securely in his bouncy seat.

I laughed. "I bet you don't care which you get because just like you, this little baby is a gift from God. You are going to be the best big brother ever!" I tickled Ryan's foot, and he giggled.

I was so proud of my child and knew without a doubt that

he would light up his brother's or sister's world. Was I still afraid of the future? Hell yes. But I chose to lean on my faith that this baby would be born healthy and that Ryan would outgrow his diseases. God had that power, and I believed He would use it. Until the pulse oximeter alarm again shook me awake from my delusion.

With Ryan back on the ventilator at the end of February, the medical staff expressed concern over the stress it would put on me and my pregnancy.

"Go home and rest," Tara suggested as I sat on the hard stool next to Ryan's bed.

"No, I'm not going to leave his side." I was adamant. "He needs me here."

"You also have to take care of yourself and your other baby."

"I know, but I need to be here with him. Where he is, I stay. It's all I know." My tear-filled eyes begged her to understand.

She sighed and handed me a tissue. "Please take breaks to get food and rest periodically in the comfy chair."

I promised her I would. But what I really wanted to do was crawl into a hole and hide, to take cover until this war was over.

I always wondered how much more Ryan could take. The question I didn't ask was: How much more could I take?

Someone once told me, "You think you love your spouse until you meet your child. Then you know what love is." There were no truer words. Ryan was the love of my life, my reason for being. My determination to protect him outweighed my need to safeguard myself. I would have given Ryan my lungs if I could have. After all, I had brought him into this world of pain and suffering. I knew it wasn't my fault, but he was created and grew inside of me, only to be emergently cut out of me. The least I could do was be with him through it all, no matter what. He deserved that from me.

Of the many challenges Ryan and I faced, being continually uprooted and forced into new environments was one of the most taxing. Our medical team understood that, so each time Ryan was admitted to the PICU, he was put into the same room, in the same bed by the window overlooking a garden below. No matter what. It was as if they saved that bed for him.

This PICU had only six beds, and almost always, Ryan was the only child being cared for while he was there. It struck me how impactful different environments can be. At the last hospital, which had been bustling with patients, Ryan was considered a burden. Here, in a quiet, more intimate setting, Ryan was a human being who was treasured. He became the star of the unit, the focal point of the doctors' and nurses' scripts, the darling of the show. He was beloved and cherished; he was special and was treated as such. Whether sedated or awake, Ryan was doted on by the staff. When I stepped out, someone always stepped in, even if just to sit with him in my absence. My little boy had taken hold of everyone's heart, and they all were emotionally invested in him, loving him as if he were their own.

As my pregnancy approached fifteen weeks, Dr. Hanson presented the option of an amniocentesis to check for prenatal genetic conditions.

"But can't that cause a miscarriage?" I asked.

"Yes," he said, "but the risk of that happening is less than one percent."

"I don't know," I said, uncertain. "I have to believe that this baby is healthy because God wouldn't do this again. I can't risk a miscarriage." I shook my head from side to side.

"Don't you think that knowing your baby is healthy would alleviate stress? You're carrying a lot on your shoulders right now, and I'm concerned that the emotional strain you're under could affect this pregnancy."

"I get that. Ryan's nurses said the same thing." I took a deep breath. "Do you promise that nothing will happen to this baby?"

I needed somebody, anybody, to make that promise to me, to alleviate my constant worry, to take control and assure me that everything would be okay. I needed to hear it even if they were lying.

"I can't promise that, but I've done hundreds of these procedures, and I do believe that you and your baby will be safe," he said with undeniable certainty.

I discussed it with John that night.

"If this baby also has Down syndrome, would we do anything about it?" he asked.

"Do you mean have an abortion? No. But it would provide time to prepare, both for us and for the prenatal care."

"What do you mean?"

"Well, if the doctors had known that Ryan had Down syndrome, they would have watched the pregnancy more closely. They would have caught the slowing of his growth in utero and could have given him medication for his lungs to develop further before birth. He still would have been born prematurely, but his lungs would have been able to function better. God forbid this baby has a genetic defect, having this knowledge may provide us with the opportunity for better medical care."

"It sounds like you think you should have the amnio," John said.

"I didn't think I wanted to, but yes, I think I should."

A week later, I watched on ultrasound as Dr. Hanson gingerly and cautiously inserted a very long needle into my uterus to withdraw fluid. I watched intently to be sure that the needle stayed far away from my baby and felt immense relief when it was withdrawn. I came away secure in the knowledge that the procedure had been safe.

"We should have the results in a couple of weeks," Dr. Hanson said. "Just take it easy for the rest of the day and you should be fine, but give me a call if you have any concerns, okay?"

"I will," I said. "Thank you."

I thought waiting two weeks for the results would be the hard part, but when abdominal cramps hit me the next morning, I went into a panicked state and called Dr. Hanson. He asked me if I had any bleeding. I didn't, but the cramps were so intense that I grew very worried. He told me to come into the office right away for an ultrasound.

I went right over. The baby was fine, but Dr. Hanson recommended bed rest for three days just to be safe.

With Ryan back at home, I reached out to our insurance company to request an increase in his in-home nursing care from sixteen to twenty-four hours so that I wouldn't have to lift him or any of the equipment, especially going up and down the stairs.

"Isn't there anyone else who can take care of your child those other eight hours?" the insurance representative asked.

I said there wasn't.

"What about your husband? Doesn't he know how?"

"No, he hasn't learned how," I stammered in shame. "It's just me."

"Your son is twenty months old. How is it that his father doesn't know how to care for him?" they said, annoyed.

"He's a good dad," I told her, "but Ryan's care is complicated, so he depends on me for it. And my husband works full time and is tired on weekends." I felt mortified, wondering if it was my fault that John hadn't learned. "Please help me. I don't want to lose this baby that I'm carrying."

She must have heard the fear in my voice because she approved my request, but only on the agreement that John "would commit to spending time with the nurses to learn how to care for his child." She added that she "wanted the time and lessons learned documented in the nurses' notes," which would ultimately be submitted to the insurance company.

Her requirement was met with resistance. "I don't want to spend my free time with the nurses," John argued when I told him.

My torso shot up from my resting position on the sofa. "Your free time? Are you kidding me right now? I'm in a constant state of emotional distress, consumed by worry and fear, desperately trying to save him at every turn...and you won't take a few hours to learn from the nurses?"

As John stormed out of the room, I shouted, "I have to protect this baby inside of me! I need your help! *We* need your help! The insurance company won't help unless you commit to this! Why is this so hard for you? He's your son!"

I was shaking with anger. John's reaction cut deep. I felt like I'd been slapped across the face by the sting of his words. I felt so alone and was saddened to feel like he would not simply step up and do whatever was necessary to help me safeguard this pregnancy. Was his free time actually more important to him than helping me take care of our children, especially under this particular emergency circumstance? Did he not care, or was he just that selfish? This was the man I'd fallen in love with; the father of my child. I didn't want to believe that any of those concepts could be true.

I was motionless on the sofa staring off into space when the nurse came down from Ryan's nursery. "Ryan is napping. Is everything okay?"

I explained what was going on with John, and she very kindly said, "He may be afraid. How about I speak with him?"

"Sure, if you want to try."

Whatever the nurse said must have worked because John ultimately conceded and apologized for putting me through that. "I'm really sorry," he said. "Whatever it takes to keep everyone safe."

I could feel his regret. "Thank you," I said and squeezed his hand.

After a few days of physical rest, my pregnancy continued with ease—physical crisis averted. My faith continued to carry me through the next few weeks as my belly expanded to the size of a basketball.

During another stay in the PICU in early April, John and I were invited to Palm Beach for a long weekend. "It'll be good for us to get away and rest for a few days," John said, but I resisted: "I can't leave Ryan, especially while he's in the hospital. No, I'm sorry, I can't go."

When I mentioned it to them, the hospital nurses and even Dr. Darby thought it was a good idea. "You know Ryan will be safe with us," he reassured me. "He's in stable condition and just needs some rest."

"And one of us will be by his side every second," Tara said coaxingly while Maria nodded silently.

Even Paula agreed. "I'll come and stay with him over the weekend. Go have some fun."

Spending time away in the warm sun did sound nice, so I finally relented. "I'll go, but I'm calling to check in several times a day."

"We wouldn't have it any other way," Maria laughed.

Those three days were medicine for my soul. Although Ryan was on my mind every minute, it wasn't in a worried, all-consuming way, but more in an "I miss my child" kind of way. It felt good to let go and let someone else take the wheel that I'd been white-knuckling. It also helped that I had faith in our team. Through their compassion, dedication, and experience over the last year, they taught me I could trust them. As my shoulders relaxed, the tension drained from my body and I could breathe freely.

Although I missed a few days with my son, his reaction upon my arrival made up for it and remains one of my favorite moments. As I peeked through his hospital door, I saw him sitting on Paula's lap in the rocking chair. I smiled as I tiptoed in to surprise them, and Ryan's eyes grew into saucers.

"Ma-ma!" he said with joyful excitement. My hands went to my mouth in surprise. It was the first time he'd ever said that word.

I scooped him up and kissed him all over his head and face, then squeezed him into my body. "Yes, Ryan, it's Mama. I missed you so, so much!"

He squealed and pushed away from my body so that he could see my face. With my arms tightly around him, he reached both hands up to my cheeks, his eyes fastened onto mine. I felt the force of his love, the biggest love I had ever felt.

In a few months, Ryan would turn two. As my pregnancy progressed, carrying him and a portable oxygen tank up and down stairs became challenging. John suggested we sell our home and move to a one-floor ranch-style house. This had been our first home and I loved it, but since we didn't know when Ryan would be strong enough to bear weight on his legs and learn to walk, I thought it made sense to at least see what was out there.

I worked with the realtor during the day and shared the information with John when he got home from work. One home, in particular, grabbed John's attention because it was a spacious ranch with easy entry. It was on a flat lot with a circular driveway in the front and a rear yard that backed up to the Watchung Reservation, offering rare privacy. We brought Ryan and Paula to see it.

"What do you think?" I asked Paula.

"It needs some work, but it's nice. The property is incredible. Great for kids!"

"What do you think, Ryan?" I asked as he sat on Paula's lap, leaning into her shoulder. I thought maybe I'd get a smile, but he seemed tired.

Paula stroked his head. "It's okay, RyRy, I think you'll like it here. Your mommy and daddy will put a swing set in the back with a slide and all kinds of fun toys for you to play with."

"You bet we will!" I said and tousled his hair.

We made an offer on the house. A few days later, it was accepted, and we put our house on the market.

Chapter Eleven

The early summer air blew through the open window as I sat with Ryan on the floor of his nursery. I could hear John outside in the driveway talking to a neighbor. We were enjoying a rare normal day, and it was bliss.

But then, out of nowhere the alarm sounded. The damn alarm!

I can't describe the panic I felt hearing that warning in the middle of one of the few normal moments we'd been able to share. I knew what the shrieking sound meant.

Ryan's oxygen levels were plunging so fast that even the extra oxygen hissing through his nasal cannula wasn't helping.

The alarm assaulted my senses. "Stop!" I screamed at the monitor, wanting to throw it against the wall.

Ryan's lips and face began to dull.

"Shit!" I yelled. "Come on, Ryan, breathe! Keep breathing!" Standing, I stuck my head out of the nursery window and called out. "Help! John, I need help!"

In the thirty seconds it took for John to run inside and upstairs, Ryan's color had improved, his oxygen saturation rate had increased, and he was back to his "normal" self.

"Jesus," John said, breathing heavily. "What happened?"

"He couldn't get air in and was turning blue." I had Ryan up against my shoulder.

"What should we do?"

"Call the doctor."

Dr. Abrams was out of the country. We called Dr. Jones.

"What happened?" he asked.

"I don't know," I said, the phone shaking in my hand. "It's like his lungs shut down."

"But he's okay now?" she asked.

"Yes, he's perfectly fine. Back to his baseline oxygen requirements, and he's breathing normally. What could have happened?"

"BPD is a complicated lung disease, and bronchospasms are a risk. This could have been an isolated incident or an indicator of something bigger. Keep a close eye on him and keep me posted."

"No!" I exclaimed. "I'm afraid. What if it happens again?"

Did he really expect me to just wait it out?

"If it happens again," he instructed me, "increase the oxygen like you did and call me back."

For the rest of the morning, I kept Ryan calm, hoping he wouldn't have another spasm, but my efforts were wasted. The alarm shrieked and he turned blue again, this time faster than he had before. This time I dialed 911.

"My baby isn't breathing!" I cried into the phone. Ryan's eyes were squeezed shut. I was on my knees, weeping at his feet, frantically begging, "Don't die on me, Ryan! Don't you dare die on me!"

Either God performed a miracle or Ryan listened to my order because the episode ended as quickly as it had begun.

I was still on the floor with Ryan when the EMS team bounded up the stairs and into the nursery. My body felt brittle. The weakness in my muscles made it difficult to stand.

"Thank God you're here," I said, breathless. "My baby has a lung disease and was in respiratory failure. He's okay now."

I pulled myself to my feet and stood frozen as the stethoscope was moved around Ryan's chest and back.

"He has good air movement in both lungs, but we should take him to the hospital just to be safe," the EMS technician said.

I wanted to wake up and start the day over. The few hours of normalcy we'd had that morning were not enough. I wanted more. I *needed* more. Taking Ryan back to the hospital was the right thing to do, but I didn't want it to be.

"I'm so sorry, Ryan. I'm so, so sorry," I said and kept him at my chest until the first responder moved him to the stretcher.

I hated everything about this disease. I hated the havoc it was wreaking on my child's body. I hated the emotional torture it created. I hated its power, its strength, and the hold it had on our lives. I hated it for robbing my child of his infancy and childhood. I hated its uncertainty. I hated it for altering our course so cruelly. And I hated the doctor whose lack of care had caused this disease to develop inside of my baby. I hated it all.

We were almost two years in at this point, and the unknowns seemed greater than they had been when Ryan was first born. Shortly after his birth, we had a diagnosis and a plan. He just had to grow, and then he'd be okay. He'd be a beautiful little boy with special needs who could focus on learning. It seemed simple. Achievable. But this? This was no longer a simple concept. This seemed insurmountable.

The complexity of his disease grew to such a degree that I began to doubt the possibility of Ryan ever having an ordinary life. I had wanted him to have the opportunity to learn how to do simple things. Like throwing a ball, chasing bubbles, running around a playground. But now we didn't even know if he would ever be able to walk, talk, or eat without a tube.

We could have dealt with Down syndrome. If only we'd be given the chance. We were more than able to provide Ryan with the tools, toys, teachings, and love he would need to develop physically and mentally. If only he could grow. If only.

I reflected on it all as we rode in the ambulance, losing hope for a normal life.

Ryan was admitted to the PICU. The spasms continued through the weekend. By Monday morning, he was intubated and back on the ventilator.

"All of the spasms over the past forty-eight hours have exhausted his heart and lungs," Dr. Darby said. "It's shocking that he recovered through as many as he did. Being on the ventilator will give his body the rest it needs."

"Is he going to pull out of it this time?" I asked.

"He's done it thus far. There's no reason to think he won't do it again." He sounded confident.

Later that day, the test results came back: sepsis. My baby had sepsis.

"I'm not going to sugarcoat it," Dr. Darby said. "Ryan is in extremely critical condition. The bacteria from his latest intestinal infection has entered his bloodstream. This has caused an inflammatory response throughout his body and is what led to the spasms in his lungs."

"He's so weak," I cried. "How is he supposed to recover this time?"

This was one more giant setback for my child who was just trying to recover from each illness, each infection, each impediment, and each mistake—none of which were of his own making. I knew that people who recovered from sepsis—if they recovered—could struggle with quality of life for years, with an increased chance of dying sooner than they would have otherwise. Would this be yet another obstacle preventing Ryan from reaching a place of stability, of normalcy?

With Ryan back on the ventilator, I sat in the hospital chapel.

"Where are you?" I asked God. "He's supposed to outgrow this disease. Why aren't you helping him? Why won't you heal him?" I didn't understand why I even had to ask. The God I believed in would want to save a child from pain.

I sat with my questions, contemplating God's answers. Maybe God hadn't yet decided the outcome of Ryan's fate. Or maybe He would tell me He was helping him. Maybe Ryan would have died already if God hadn't been helping.

Feeling guilty for questioning Him, I pressed my hands together in prayer.

"I'm sorry, God. I'm just so scared and tired. I need Ryan to be okay, and we desperately need you to make that happen. Please heal him. *Please.*"

Dr. Darby and Dr. Abrams were standing at Ryan's bedside when I returned to his room.

"How's he doing?" I asked.

"He's stable for now," Dr. Darby answered.

The "for now" always rocked me. At any moment, Ryan's

heart or lungs could stop working. Then what?

Dr. Abrams pulled the stool closer to Ryan's bed and motioned for me to sit. I obeyed.

"How are you feeling?" he asked me.

"Physically fine. Emotionally, not so much."

"How many weeks pregnant are you now?"

"Twenty-seven," I answered, staring at the numbers on the ventilator screen.

"I know you well enough not to ask you to go home and rest since you won't leave Ryan's side," he said, "but please be sure to eat and move around periodically. And be sure to let your OB/GYN know that Ryan is back in the hospital." He gently squeezed my shoulder.

Nodding, I popped open the music player and inserted the lullaby tape, holding tightly to Ryan's limp hand as the soothing rhythmic melody drifted through the room.

Would I ever get used to seeing my baby being kept alive by a machine? Would I have to? Could I handle it? I was doubtful. The grief I felt coursing through my body each time I had to watch my son suffer was agonizing. Even though friends and family always commented on how strong I was, I knew that there was just a single thread holding me together that could unravel at any moment. That thread was Ryan. Drained, I leaned forward on the bed and lay my head on my arms next to Ryan's still form. I stayed that way for the next five days.

* * *

The ventilator seemed to have worked its magic. The paralytic and the sedation were weaned, and we watched Ryan's body come back to life. I breathed relief.

With the tube still in his mouth, Ryan smiled up at me.

"Hi, RyRy, I've missed that smile and those beautiful eyes."

"He seems ready to be extubated," Dr. Darby told me. "Go wait in the hall and I'll come get you when we're done."

"I'll be right back, sweetie," I said and kissed Ryan's forehead, smiling as I exited.

About ten minutes passed before Dr. Darby came to get me. "Ryan isn't breathing as well as I had hoped," he told me. "I'd like you to come see."

"That can't be right," I said, racing through the PICU door.

His poor little face. Ryan's eyes were wide as if asking, "What's happening? Why can't I breathe?" He was trying but was unable to sustain his breaths, his chest sinking deeply each time he inhaled.

"I think it's best if we reintubate him and give his body more rest," Dr. Darby recommended.

I dropped my head and moaned. Mustering every ounce of strength I had, I gently squeezed Ryan's hand and looked into his face. "RyRy, you're going to rest for a little bit longer. Mommy will be back by your side in a few minutes, okay?"

I pressed a tissue to my face as I left and walked the few feet to the hallway, where I slid my back down the wall, hugged my knees to my chest, and wept. All I wanted was to have my child healthy and at home. Was that too much to ask? Just a month earlier, we'd been nestled at home laughing and playing. Ryan was making strides in his therapies, and we were planning for the future. Were we wasting our time?

I hated myself for even contemplating the answer to that question, but the never-ending whiplash of emotions was becoming unbearable and I was furious at the "one step forward, two steps back" routine. We weren't just experiencing ups and downs. We were ascending to the highest peak of possibilities, hopes, and dreams…only to be smacked off into the craters of Hell. Because watching your child suffer over and over again is just that: Hell.

The door opened and Dr. Darby put his hand out to help me up. "You can come back in now."

"He's never failed an attempt to be extubated. What does it mean?" I asked.

"His body just wasn't ready. We'll try again in another week. Try not to worry."

Throughout the next week, even though Ryan continued to be plagued with positive blood cultures and fevers, all signs pointed to another possible successful extubation. Once again, I left the room to wait.

After a while, Maria came out into the hallway with a smile. "He's doing okay."

"Oh, thank God!"

Ryan's beautiful brown eyes were open once again. Although exhausted, he seemed stable.

"Welcome back, sweetie," I said, holding his hand as Dr. Darby, Maria, and I watched his respirations.

About fifteen minutes later, Ryan's breaths became slightly shallower, the chest retractions a bit deeper.

"No, no, no, Ryan. C'mon, you can do this, sweetie!" I kissed his forehead and held his hand more tightly. "Ryan, breathe better. I know you can breathe better. Please, baby, please," I begged.

The fear in his eyes shredded me as he struggled to inhale.

He was trying so hard, but his efforts were no match for the infections ravaging his body.

Maria drew blood to determine the level of CO_2 in his blood. The number came back frighteningly high, proving that his broken body was unable to remove it with his shallow, rapid breaths.

"Susan, I have to reintubate him," Dr. Darby said softly.

"No!" I wailed. "C'mon, Ryan! You need to breathe! Please breathe! You have to breathe, Ryan!"

Maria put her hand on my shoulder. I clung to Ryan, unable to let him go, sobbing over his chest before nodding my head and stepping back.

I went out to my car and cried for a very long time, screaming and pounding the steering wheel, reliving every trauma like a slideshow: the emergency birth, the fear of having to bury my baby in a tiny casket, the development of the lung disease, the multitudes of wires and tubes, the numerous consultations and hospitalizations, the countless infections and intubations, the questionable ethics and malicious behavior of medical professionals, the multiple surgeries, the abundance of medications including narcotics, the development of the heart disease, the rivers of tears cried and the horrors witnessed. It broke me to think that after all our son had endured, all that we had fought for, all the joy he had brought to our lives, these two failed extubation attempts could kill him. What was it all for?

A kick in my belly brought me back to the present. I leaned back in the driver's seat, keenly aware of the other life depending on me and my need to pull it together. After regaining my strength and composure, I opened the car door and dragged my body back to Ryan.

"I'm sorry," I said to Dr. Darby and Maria. "I know you're just trying to help him."

"Don't apologize," Maria said and hugged me. "We know how much you love him and how deeply this is hurting you."

"I'd like to check your blood pressure," Dr. Darby said, a worried look on his face.

"No, I'm fine."

"Let's check it just to be sure," Maria said and wrapped the cuff around my arm.

The reading was 120 over 80.

"You must have some kind of angel looking out for you," Dr. Darby said in surprise.

I went back to rubbing Ryan's head, holding his hand, massaging him, and reading to him. It was in these moments that I wished I could sing.

Dr. Darby was still hopeful for another extubation attempt, but Ryan became intensely agitated, moaning and thrashing side to side. Higher doses of the paralytic and sedatives were required to keep him calm. At the same time, the ventilator settings were increasing, and his lungs were showing more signs of infection.

Hope had died. Despair swelled within me, forcing the air out of my lungs. "We're not going to be able to get him off the ventilator, are we?"

Dr. Darby shook his head. "No. I'm sorry. I know that's not what you want to hear."

"Is he dying?" I could barely get the words out.

"He's very sick. His organs are getting weaker."

My throat tightened and I couldn't swallow. My skin turned clammy.

"You look pale. Sit down," Maria said and ushered me to the chair.

"This can't be happening. We brought him here to get better, not to die, not to be stuck on a ventilator!" I yelled at them from the edge of the chair.

Dr. Darby flinched, pain etched on his face. I knew my anger was misdirected. The doctors had done their best to give Ryan a beautiful life, and they'd done it with purpose. Not only did they care, but they loved us. Our pain was theirs. As I realized the depths of Dr. Darby's sorrow, my voice softened.

"This is my baby, my little boy. He was supposed to grow, and be happy, and do all the things little boys do. We were supposed to be a family." Defeated, I sat back in the chair as sobs shook my body. "He's supposed to be a big brother," I whispered and touched my belly.

Maria sat on the arm of the chair and pulled me to her. "It's okay," she said, "let it out."

I cried for Ryan, for me, for my husband, and for the baby inside of me. I thought my love for Ryan was my best guide, my maternal instincts the compass with which to navigate his care. Had I been wrong? Plagued with grief, I felt like I was free-falling down the side of a cliff waiting to hit bottom.

For the next three weeks, I sat and prayed. Ryan's fevers were constant, and blood cultures continued to be positive for a bacterial infection. It was now mid-July, and I was thirty-two weeks pregnant. Ryan had been intubated for over a month with high ventilator settings and continued to struggle with frequent episodes of bronchospasms and fevers. As new life grew inside of me, I felt like Ryan was slipping away. I didn't know how to reconcile that. He was my whole heart, and I felt like I was watching him die. How was I supposed to feel joy for the impending birth of his brother?

Dr. Darby and Dr. Abrams scheduled a meeting with me and John to discuss Ryan's future course of treatment. Sensing that the treatment would include a tracheotomy, I sat with my arms crossed, defying them to even mention the word.

"Don't say it," I begged.

"It's clear we're not going to be able to get Ryan off the ventilator. We think a tracheotomy would be the best next step," Dr. Abrams said and looked encouragingly at me.

"No, please, no," I said, looking from one doctor to the other. I was a mixed-up cocktail of seething anger and incapacitating sadness.

Dr. Darby shifted in his chair. "It's our only option."

"Can't we just leave him intubated until he gets stronger?" John asked.

"His condition has deteriorated to such a degree that we're certain he's not going to get stronger," Dr. Abrams answered.

This was the nightmare ending, the outcome I had feared the most: Ryan being dependent on life support and suffering for the rest of his life, however short or long that might be. My dreams of rainbows and butterflies vanished.

"Ryan won't want this. In my heart, I *know* that he would not want this," I insisted.

"What's the alternative?" John asked.

I looked at Dr. Darby, wondering if he would share that answer with John.

"The alternative is to discontinue treatment by taking Ryan off the ventilator now."

"But wouldn't he die if we did that?" John asked, perplexed.

"Given how his body responded during the two previous attempts to extubate him, yes."

Our little boy had come so far and had fought so hard to survive. Was it really coming down to this? A bolt of fear shot through my body. Was I considering removing my baby from life support? Could I actually do it? And what would happen if I pushed for it? It would mean I was asking for my child to die. What kind of a mother does that? Would John ever forgive me? Could I ever forgive myself? In my heart, I knew I would be saving Ryan from more suffering. But to cause his death by unplugging a machine? I didn't know if I was brave enough to force that on my own.

"We need to have some conversations and get more information," I said.

"Of course. You know we're here to help in your decision. Whatever you need," Dr. Abrams reassured us.

I went back to Ryan's bedside and John went to work. Maria was suctioning his endotracheal tube. "Are you okay?" she asked me.

"No. They want to trach him, Maria."

"I know. How do you feel about it?"

"I think it would only make him suffer more. Every time we do something to him, whether it's a new hole or another foreign object surgically placed in his body, it causes trouble. How is a trach going to be any different? You know as well as I do how much Ryan hates being on the vent and how much he hates suctioning. How the hell will he be able to handle a trach?" I paced the room with heavy steps.

"You have an impossible, difficult decision to make," she said.

The next day, I asked for the opinion of the resident who helped in his treatment.

"Do you think a trach will cause him more pain," I asked her, "or do you think it will help?"

She sighed. "It becomes a quality-of-life issue, and only you know what that quality is like when Ryan is at home and feeling well," she said, putting the unwanted ball back in my court.

I let that sink in. Her words made sense, but I knew that this surgery would change that quality of life. I wasn't even convinced that a trach would ever get Ryan back home. He had been so fragile since birth, and it seemed infection always found its way into his body. A trach would be just another port of entry for the bacteria. If I knew that to be true, how could the doctor not know?

That night at home, I sat cross-legged on the sofa with Jake at my feet.

John handed me a cup of tea. "Here, it's chamomile."

"Thanks," I said, unconsciously massaging my protruding belly.

We were about to close on our new house and move in even though we hadn't yet had luck selling our current one. Boxes and packing supplies surrounded us, reminding me of the workload ahead.

"It's not fair," I said. "Ryan doesn't deserve this. He's just a sweet little boy who only wants to be loved and to live his life. That's all I ever wanted for him." My fingers brushed away the falling tears.

"I know, me too, but by doing the tracheotomy, we're giving him a chance to have that."

"No. We'd be causing him more suffering. I can't explain

how I know it, but I do."

"We have to at least try it. The doctors said it's the only way to attempt to one day wean him off the vent."

"I know what they said, and I know they mean well, but they're wrong. This surgery will only cause him more pain. John, I know you love Ryan and want the best for him, but you haven't been around to see him. To actually *see* him. When Ryan has been at his lowest, at his weakest, at his most fragile state, you've either been at work or traveling for work, or traveling for family events."

My frustration grew, and I felt I might be pushing too hard, but I couldn't stop.

"For the last two years, Ryan has spent seventy-five percent of his life in hospitals, most of that time in critical condition on a vent. I've been the one to sit at his bedside loving him, caring for him, making sure he wouldn't feel alone, all the while begging and bargaining with God to make him better. *I* did that, so I need you to support me in this."

"Look," John said, "we've had different roles. I have to go to work to make money and keep our health insurance active. That doesn't mean I don't get a say in what happens here!"

I felt like I'd been slapped.

There's a saying that most disagreements are caused by diverse perceptions that create different realities. Were my actions or inactions responsible for our current state of division? For two years I went along with the role of being the sole parental caregiver to Ryan. I didn't ask for more from my husband other than during the required bed rest. I gave him silent permission to act as he saw fit, including leaving me alone to deal with medical emergencies. He had depended on me over these last two years for all medical information and the status of our son's condition, yet I'd allowed him to feel that he was just as involved in Ryan's care as I was. Was it no wonder, then, that he couldn't understand my position now when it came to Ryan's treatment?

For the next few weeks, Dr. Darby and John pushed for the trach. Although many of the nurses agreed with me, they had no role in this decision. It was me against Dr. Darby and John. I felt very alone and angry that I couldn't successfully convey my convictions.

We sought counsel through our church minister and extensively researched the pros and cons of trachs—the training and care required, living with a trach—and reached out through the web for people who'd been through this with their own child. The responses were varied. Some had good outcomes, others had tragic endings. But these stories of strangers had no bearing on my truth, on my knowledge of what my son needed. Ryan had his own story, and it was a book that I was present in on every page. There was no way in hell that I would agree to a trach.

Dr. Darby scheduled a meeting with the hospital bioethics committee to evaluate our options as Ryan's parents. John and I waited in the hallway as our doctors, a few of our nurses, and members of the committee who were unfamiliar with our child gathered in a meeting room to review Ryan's case. We were, once again, in a situation where a medical institution would possibly be deciding the fate of our child.

I was now in the thirty-sixth week of my pregnancy, and my body felt like a rope unraveling, my nerves frayed to the tips of my fingers and toes.

The conference room door opened, and we were invited

inside. I wobbled in wearing a long yellow maternity dress and looked around at the friendly faces of those who loved me and Ryan. Comforted by their smiles, I released my grip on John's hand and sat, feeling a bit calmer.

The chairman of the committee, an elderly doctor from another hospital, led the discussion. "We had a case last year of a ten-year-old boy who became ventilator-dependent following a car accident. His injuries prohibited his ability to breathe on his own for an extensive period of time, leading to the need for a tracheotomy. As he recovered, he was able to be weaned off the vent and is now leading a full life. There is no reason to believe your son will not have the same outcome."

There were no similarities between that child's case and Ryan's. The chairman may as well have been holding an apple in one hand and an orange in the other claiming both fruits were the same.

I raised my hand to speak, and he nodded. "What were your thoughts when you saw our son?" I asked him.

He cleared his throat. "I haven't seen your son."

My eyes widened. "Then on what are you basing your opinion?"

"We've done a thorough review of your son's case, and since he has full brain activity, it is my opinion that the trach is his only option."

"And what about his quality of life? What are your thoughts on that?"

It was clear from the look in his eyes that he didn't appreciate me challenging him. "I've provided you with my guidance and knowledge based on my extensive experience as a doctor. Your son will need the tracheotomy."

His ego was staggering. My mouth opened in shock. He stood, and that was it; the end of the discussion.

"How dare he?" I hissed at John. "Who does he think he is?" I stood and followed the chairman. "Excuse me," I said, tapping his shoulder.

Even though he was standing before a very pregnant woman, he regarded me with a hardened look on his face.

"Before you leave," I said, "why don't you come see my son and witness what I have seen nearly every day for the past two years?"

"As I said, I don't need to, and I'm late for another meeting," he said and walked down the hallway without a care in the world.

"You should be ashamed of yourself!" I shouted.

He didn't flinch. I wanted to hurl something at his back. John held onto me as we walked back to Ryan's room.

"What was that?" I asked Dr. Darby.

"That did not go as I'd hoped, and I'm very disappointed by the lack of support shown to you," he replied.

"I felt like we were ambushed! He doesn't even know Ryan. He didn't even bother to see him, and he thinks he can tell me what my child needs? What the outcome will be?" I was shaking with anger.

"Please sit down," Maria said. She motioned me to the chair and handed me a cup of water. She looked at Dr. Darby. "That didn't help them try to resolve this."

"No, it didn't. Let me make another call," Dr. Darby said.

In the meantime, Ryan was still lying lifeless, paralyzed and sedated for his seventh week. What was I, as his mother, supposed to do now?

Chapter Twelve

The call Dr. Darby made was to the director of medical ethics at a children's hospital in our state, a woman who he said was "fair and compassionate." As it turned out, she was also a mother. I met Dr. Stanton for the first time at Ryan's bedside.

"He's beautiful," she said to me.

"He is."

He looked peaceful, but we both knew otherwise. The medications hid the truth.

I saw a flicker of sorrow in her face. It matched mine. "Would you like to get some air?" she asked me.

"Sure." I stroked Ryan's cheek with my fingers. "RyRy, Mommy will be back soon."

We sat outside on a bench under a tree.

"Tell me about your son."

I stared at my feet. "He's amazing. He's a sweet, loving little boy who doesn't deserve what's happening to him." I couldn't say the words without crying.

Dr. Stanton sat patiently and listened as I shared Ryan's

history. "Sounds like you all have been through a great deal of trauma," she said. I nodded. "Dr. Darby believes that a tracheotomy is the best path," she continued, "but he said you disagree. Can you tell me why?"

"Because Ryan has suffered so much, and I know he wouldn't want this."

"The alternative is to end life-sustaining treatment, which means your son will die. Are you prepared for that?"

I contemplated the question. I had witnessed my child almost die multiple times. Did that make me more prepared for his eventual death? I was doubtful, as the depth of my recurring terror and grief never lessened. The thought of burying my son sent shivers down my spine, the finality of his life impossible to fathom. So, no, I was not prepared for his death.

Dr. Stanton spoke with John the next day, and he told her that he supported the decision to give Ryan a tracheotomy. After their conversation, we scheduled a meeting between the three of us.

"This would be an extraordinarily difficult and emotional decision even if you both agreed," Dr. Stanton told us. "Not agreeing makes it that much harder. But I've heard you both speak with great love for your son, and it's clear you each want what's best for him. At this point, there are three options: Leave Ryan intubated indefinitely or until he dies, withdraw him from the ventilator now, at which point he will die, or do the tracheotomy. No decision is wrong. The question is, what is best for your son? We don't know the answer to that, but here's the thing. Unless you both agree to end life-sustaining treatment, the only option is to perform the tracheotomy."

I felt hatred toward my husband and I resented that Dr.

Stanton gave equal weight to our opinions, as if they had both been formed with the same information. I felt strongly that John was deciding Ryan's fate without first-hand knowledge of what Ryan had endured on a daily basis. It was as if a juror were deciding a person's guilt or innocence without having been present at trial.

"I understand what you're saying, but John is wrong. This will not save Ryan. It won't only prolong his suffering. It will cause *catastrophic* suffering."

I left the building in disgust, aching over what lay ahead for Ryan and livid that I couldn't stop it. I felt like I was screaming in silence. My words didn't seem to matter, nor did my love for my child. God knew I didn't want Ryan to leave us. I couldn't bear the thought of living in this world without him. But I also wanted to shield him from additional pain and a horrible quality of life. Now I was being given no choice but to bow to the powers that be—two men who thought they knew better than me, the child's mother, a mother whose heart beat solely for that child.

In just two days, Ryan would get a trach and a new port-a-cath. This was early August, and we had just moved into our new home. Ryan's new home.

"I know this isn't what you want, but let's see how it goes," Dr. Darby said, his tone encouraging. "He may surprise you."

I was not optimistic.

On the day of surgery, I was just three and a half weeks away from my scheduled C-section. John and I walked alongside Ryan's bed as he was wheeled down to the surgical floor. His body was lifeless, the mood somber as Dr. Darby, Dr. Abrams, and Maria walked with us. All of our faces showed the same combination of fear, sadness, and an intense desire to help Ryan.

Stopping at the doors to the operating room, I made one last-ditch effort. "Please don't do this to him," I pleaded with Dr. Darby. "Look at him. Think about how much he has already suffered. What if this was your child?"

He looked down at his feet.

"John, please don't let them do this to Ryan. Please!"

"It's the only option."

"It's time to take him in," the nurse said.

"No, please no." I would not let go of Ryan's hand.

"Susan, you need to let go," Dr. Darby urged.

I had spent the last two years holding onto Ryan so tightly, holding onto my hope for his future, to our dreams of being a family. *Letting go* meant no longer protecting him. As long as I had breath in me, I would never stop protecting him.

"You don't realize what you're about to do to him." I looked from one face to another, hoping for an awakening in one of them to change course and stand beside me. Nothing.

How the hell did I have no power?

As they pulled the bed through the doors, I lost my grip on Ryan's hand. I collapsed against the wall. John stepped forward to comfort me, but I put my arm up to stop him. "No!" I felt any solace he attempted was a betrayal. He had been partially responsible for this latest trauma being forced upon both me and Ryan. I didn't want him touching me.

Realizing this, Maria drew me to her and held me as I cried. "Let's get you up to a room to rest," she said.

I walked lifelessly through the halls, stopping in an empty room near the PICU where she said we could rest.

I lay frozen in the fetal position on the bed, in terror that

Ryan would die, but also that he would live and be miserable. I could never describe the depth of my love for him—so much that I didn't want to subject him to more suffering through this surgery. Did that make me a horrible person? What kind of mother wouldn't do everything possible to save her child, no matter what? I found myself doubting my convictions that I knew what was best. Was I being selfless or selfish? I had no answers, and I had no prayers left.

I could hear John on the phone out in the hallway. Had he chosen this moment to get some work done, or was he updating the family on Ryan? I became obsessed wondering which it was. Frustrated by not knowing, I turned onto my other side, facing away from the door. I imagined Ryan lying on the surgical table being prepped and pumped full of drugs. At what point would they cut the hole into my son's throat? Had they already done it? Would he wake up?

Feeling the wetness of my tears on the pillow, I turned it over onto the dry side. Drained, I closed my eyes.

I woke to a gentle shake of my shoulder.

"They're bringing him back up," Maria said as she helped me up from the bed.

"He made it through?"

She nodded.

I stood in the doorway while John stood across the hall. When I heard the wheels of the stretcher rounding the corner, I stepped hesitantly toward it as soon as it appeared.

"How is he?" I asked the surgeon.

"The surgery went well. There were no complications."

Equal amounts of relief and sorrow washed over me. For the first time since Ryan was just a few weeks old, his face was free of tubes. There was no nasal cannula and no endotracheal tube. Seeing his swollen face unencumbered was the one bright moment. Then I saw the tube protruding from his throat. I welled with deep sadness. How would he feel when he realized what had been done to him?

Once Ryan was settled back in the PICU, Dr. Darby and Dr. Abrams discussed their treatment plan. I felt hamstrung and had no choice but to be a team player. They believed they could help Ryan, so I tried to trust in their belief to see it through.

"We're going to keep Ryan heavily sedated for the next week and a half and then slowly try to wean him off the ventilation," Dr. Darby said.

"Do you expect that to work?" John asked.

"Ryan is severely addicted to all of the drugs that have kept him sedated over the last few months, so it's not going to be a quick or easy process," Dr. Abrams added. "He will experience intense withdrawal symptoms while trying to gain the strength to breathe, so it's going to be hard for him."

"He's just a baby and he'll be going through withdrawal," I moaned. Numb and exhausted, I left the room in silence and went home to unpack.

In three weeks I would be delivering my baby, and there was so much to do. I looked around at the boxes that surrounded me. Where to start? I grabbed a pair of scissors and opened box after box of dishes, glasses, pots, and pans. I studied the cabinets trying to figure out the best place for each. Overwhelmed, I walked down the hallway to Ryan's room. Boxes were stacked there also. The demands facing me felt impossible. I hadn't anticipated feeling pulled to such an extent, and I prayed Ryan didn't feel abandoned. Chaos and guilt suffocated me. Having accomplished nothing, I grabbed my car keys and headed back to where I belonged: with Ryan.

As I sat at his side for the next week and a half, his fever spiked and his vent settings had to be increased. Ryan was getting worse, not better.

"Susan," Dr. Darby told me, "he's very weak. We need to re-paralyze him."

An emptiness flooded through me. A new life was growing inside of me, yet I felt dead. I wanted to say, "I told you so," but instead I walked out of the room feeling like the ground was shifting beneath me. It was as if I could feel the cracks but didn't know whether to avoid them or allow them to swallow me up.

As Ryan's second birthday approached, I wondered if he would be awake to celebrate. I stroked his cheek. "RyRy, it's your birthday next week. You're going to be two. Such a big boy, and soon you'll be a big brother. I know you're really tired, but can you try to get better for Mommy, sweetie? I'd love to see your beautiful smile on your birthday."

Improvements were evident a few days later. Ryan's fevers were gone, and as the sedation was reduced, he was less agitated, seemingly adjusting to the feeling and placement of the trach.

My baby was coming back to life.

On August 24, Ryan turned two. The staff planned a pizza party in his honor. Balloons of all shapes and colors covered the ceiling, with bright ribbons dangling from each. Presents were stacked on the windowsill, and the most beautiful cake rested on a table.

"Wow, you guys did all this?" I asked, my hands crossed over my heart.

"It's a special day," Dr. Darby said and hugged me.

I was overcome by their love.

"Sit," one of the nurses said, pulling the rocking chair close to the bed.

They gingerly placed Ryan in my arms. It had been over two months since I'd held him, and he was much heavier. As I struggled to get him into a comfortable position on my giant belly, I realized that I hadn't been this afraid and nervous to hold my child since the first time I'd held him in the NICU. Sensing my unease, the nurses jumped in to assist, propping a pillow at my side to give Ryan more support.

"Is that better, RyRy?" I said and nestled him closer to me.

He was immobile and expressionless but his eyes were open, which was the greatest gift of all that day. As the minutes passed, I felt lighter, a feeling I thought had vanished forever. Holding him again felt like home.

One nurse presented the cake to Ryan and shocked us by taking his hand and pressing it into the cake. "Every child has to smash the cake!" she said. She held Ryan's hand over me and I giggled as frosting dripped onto my dress.

"Happy birthday, Ryan," Dr. Abrams said as he arrived. He kissed Ryan's head, rubbed his cheek, and gave me a hug and kiss. "What is this mess?" he asked as he cleaned Ryan's hands and wiped the drops of frosting off my dress. I considered this to be a display of rare and exceptional dedication and love.

Gifts were opened, many coinciding with our plan to decorate Ryan's room in our new house in a nautical theme in primary colors. I opened a box to find a beautiful hand-carved wooden fisherman wearing a rust-colored rain jacket and blue hat, accompanied by a white and blue round frame designed like a lifesaver with the words *first mate.*

"Oh, how amazing!" I exclaimed.

"You're still planning on doing a nautical theme, right?" asked Brenda, Ryan's home nurse.

"Yes," I said, smiling gratefully, "and these gifts are so special."

"Well, I hope you like it, Ryan. It's for your new room, and you're the first mate," Brenda said and kissed Ryan's cheek.

"Oh, he will! He'll be grabbing it and hitting his brother with it," I joked. "Or, this could be your new doctor-whacker, Ryan." I held the fisherman in front of him, and he reached to feel it. Laughter filled the room.

"You're going to have such a fancy room now!" Brenda said to Ryan, then turned to me. "Did you get a chance to decorate it yet?"

"Not yet," I answered. I was afraid to decorate it for fear that Ryan would never get to see it.

Dr. Darby handed me a piece of cake and rubbed Ryan's head. Paula's gift was a large red, blue, yellow, and green geometric-shaped mobile with triangles, circles, and squares that spun over Ryan's bed. "This can go in your new room at home, RyRy," she said as she squeezed his cheeks.

I smiled through it all while nervously glancing up at the monitors at every opportunity to check Ryan's heart rate, oxygen levels, and blood pressure. I hid the fear that consumed me. I'm glad I did. That day could be described with only one word: love.

Ten days later, I arrived at the hospital to deliver my baby via C-section. My first stop was Ryan's bedside to say good morning to my firstborn. I was ecstatic to see his eyes open.

"Hi, baby boy," I said as I kissed his head.

Ryan grabbed Floppy Fellow as a tear fell from his eye. Why the tear, I wondered. Was he in pain, or was he sad that I was about to bring his baby brother into the world and he couldn't be with us to celebrate?

"Aww, sweetie." I wiped the tear from his cheek.

A squeaking grunting sound was coming from his trach. He dropped Floppy Fellow and put his hands together.

"I love you, sweet potato. I love you so much." I placed kisses all over his head. "I'll see you tomorrow, okay? I love you, I love you."

I kissed his cheek. I didn't want to leave him.

He clapped his hands as if to say, "I'm going to be a big brother!"

I set Floppy Fellow and Elmo next to him. "I love you, RyRy," I whispered in his ear, breathing in his scent.

I hated walking away from him that morning. It was a surreal torture to also feel excited about meeting my new child. It felt like I was betraying Ryan.

John had the video camera focused on me as I said goodbye to Ryan, and then again as I sat on the bed in my hospital gown waiting to be taken into surgery.

"How about a close-up?" John asked.

"How about not?" I responded with half a smile, then added as I looked into the camera, "Ryan, I promise you I will never let another IV go into your body. That really hurt!"

"Your mommy has a beer belly," John joked into the video camera.

"Looks like Aunt Paula might win the bet with her eight-pound guess. We're not sure," I added. "RyRy, I love you! Your daddy will show this video to you. I'll give you a little brother in about an hour." I blew a kiss into the camera, waved goodbye, and motioned "I love you" in sign language.

Once the epidural was administered and the catheter inserted, it was time. The surgical nurse wheeled me into the operating room with John at my side.

"You ready?" Dr. Hanson asked.

I nodded.

"Okay, here we go."

I held my breath as Dr. Hanson asked for the scalpel.

"Take deep breaths. Everything is okay. Just breathe," the nurse said, trying to comfort me. Did she know that my other son was down the hall in the PICU on a ventilator?

I felt the hiss of oxygen coursing through the cannula penetrate my nasal cavity. *So this is what it felt like for Ryan,* I thought. But for him, it was 24/7. Not fun. I wished he could be with me so I could tell him that I understood now.

Tomorrow, I thought. *I will tell him tomorrow.*

My thoughts shifted the moment I heard the sound of a soft whimper followed by an intense wail.

"He's out," the nurse announced.

"Is he okay?" I asked, my voice insistent.

"Ten fingers, ten toes. He's perfect."

The same tears that had soaked my pillow when Ryan was born now reappeared.

"Just getting him cleaned up," the nurse said.

Within minutes, they put my son into my arms, and I cradled him to my chest and held on tightly. "Hello, my child. Welcome to the world." I stared at him in wonderment—no tubes, no lines, no monitors.

So this is what it's like, I thought.

Love surged through me.

"He's so beautiful," I said to John.

"You both are," he said.

The nurse reached to take the baby to the newborn nursery to perform the post-birth exam.

"Can't I hold him just a bit longer, please?" I begged.

"You'll be in recovery for a bit. We'll bring him to you as soon as you're settled in your room," she said. Her eyes were soft as she lifted him.

She must know, I thought.

It wasn't long before I was wheeled into a private room and quickly joined by Paula, Maria, and Tara.

"Congratulations!" Tara said. "Give us the details."

"Eight pounds, six ounces. A big boy. Paula wins the bet." I yawned. "How's Ryan?"

"He's doing fine," Maria said. "No changes. We told him you'd be back to see him tomorrow."

"I already miss him and it's only been a few hours. How am I going to manage this?"

"We'll all help," Paula said. "Let's celebrate this birth."

My melancholy was replaced with joy when the nurse wheeled my baby in. The connection when I held him was undeniable. His eyes bore into mine as if he knew he was giving my broken heart a respite from the pain.

"I just want to squeeze you so tight, but I can't right now." I nuzzled my cheek next to his. My aches for Ryan were constant, but my body and my mind needed a happy place in which to rest. I embraced the calm of the maternity ward with my baby.

The next morning, John wheeled me down to visit Ryan. Another child, an adolescent boy, was in the next bed, his mother by his side. This was a first. Ryan had never had a roommate at this hospital.

Our eyes met, and I felt a shared sorrow.

What's wrong with her son? I wondered.

Still quite stiff and sore from the surgery, John helped me up from the chair and supported me while I stood over Ryan.

"Hi, RyRy, you have a baby brother. His name is Christian. Did Daddy show you the video of me saying hi?"

Ryan's eyes were vacant.

"He had a tough night," the nurse shared.

"Can you pull the stool close to the bed?" I asked. "I'm going to sit with him awhile."

"You sure? You just had surgery, and this stool is far from comfortable."

"Yes, I'm sure." My next round of pain medication wasn't due for another three hours. I could handle a little pain, especially given what Ryan was enduring.

I caught the other mother glancing over at us. "Did you just have a baby?" she asked.

"Yes, yesterday. Another boy."

"Congratulations." She smiled, but I saw unmistakable loss in her eyes.

Over the next three days, I shared my time between my hospital room and Ryan's room. I couldn't bring Ryan down to Christian's room, and I couldn't bring Christian to Ryan because of the risk of infection. I needed two of me. So did my boys.

Then the dreaded day of discharge came, and I was once again forced to leave Ryan behind in the hospital.

"Here we go again," I said to Paula, my throat dry as my voice cracked.

"I know, this truly sucks," she said, rubbing my back. "You go spend time with Ryan, and I'll take all these gifts home."

We embraced when she left. I went to Ryan's room. He was propped up in bed watching *Sesame Street*. Maria and Tara were at his bedside.

"Aww, you're both here," I smiled, happy to see them both with Ryan.

"We know this is going to be hard, and we want you to know we'll be here with Ryan for the rest of the day."

I opened my arms to hug them but stopped abruptly when the alarm sounded. Ryan started coughing. His trach had come detached. His face was so swollen from steroids that his inflated cheeks rested on his chest. He no longer had a neck, making it hard for the trach to stay in place. I winced as Maria quickly reattached it to his throat.

Ryan grimaced and grunted whenever he tried to move. He tried to reach for a toy but was too weak. He tried to clap his hands but couldn't get them together. His swollen body was like a straitjacket restricting all movement.

If he could have spoken, I think he would have asked, "Why are you doing this to me?"

As I prepared myself emotionally to leave, words escaped me. What was I supposed to tell him? My choices seemed to be "I'm abandoning you to take your brother home" or "I love you but I can no longer be here with you."

My healthy baby was down the hall waiting to go home. My dying child was here. What was I supposed to do? Why was I supposed to choose? I loved both with every cell in my body.

"Christian is ready to be discharged," John said as he came to get me.

My "mom" armor cracked, sending splintering lines down my body. I pressed both of Ryan's hands against my lips. "You, my precious child, are my heart. I love you." My eyes were pleading with him to feel the truth of my words. "I'll be back soon."

I kissed him goodbye and walked out of the room, leaving half of my heart with him.

The same video camera that I'd stared into when I was discharged after Ryan's birth was once again in front of me. The same forced smile was captured. The part of me that cradled my baby in my arms was joyful, but the other part that was leaving Ryan in the hospital was lost in grief. As I settled into the car, I felt unsure if I was heading home or leaving home.

Our home had been purchased for Ryan, but we were carrying Christian into it without Ryan there to welcome his baby brother. Memories of Ryan in this home had not yet been created, and I shivered at the foreboding feeling of his absence as I entered the foyer.

Christian was asleep in the car seat and Paula was in the kitchen. Jake bounded up to greet us.

"Hi, Jake, I missed you!" I knelt and hugged his neck, feeling a wet tongue in my ear.

Paula leaned out of the kitchen doorway. "I just made some tea. Would you like a cup?"

"Sure, thanks."

"How'd it go?" she asked.

"Horrible," I said and sat, shaking my head. "My poor child. How many more times will I have to walk away from him?"

I was in a fog those first few days at home. I wandered around the house not knowing where to go or what to do. I was used to waking up and spending all day at the hospital. Now, when I woke, I called the PICU to check on Ryan and then tended to Christian's needs. I felt like a spinning top on an uneven surface, bobbing and weaving as I tried to grapple with the juxtaposition of the health and needs of my two boys.

The ease with which I was able to care for Christian felt foreign. I had asked Dr. Jones if I should have a home monitor for Christian "just in case." Trauma lived deep within me, and I couldn't grasp the fact that most babies can safely breathe on their own. When Christian wasn't eating or crying, I was checking to be sure he was breathing, looking for any sign of respiratory distress.

As I adjusted to having a healthy child at home, Ryan's struggles worsened. Attempts to wean him from the ventilator were halted. High fevers consumed his body, and MRSA grew from his trach. Multiple tests were done to check for other sources of infection: abdominal ultrasound, two echocardiograms, several cultures, and even a gallium scan that checked for anything inflammatory or fungal. All came back negative. All antibiotics and antifungal medications were halted to see if his fevers were drug-related, but the fevers continued—103, 104, even as high as 105.

My visits with Ryan went from every single day to every other day and weekends. He was miserable. He lay in bed thrashing his head from side to side, grunting, and grinding his teeth. He grimaced and now hated being touched. He flinched when I tried to hold his hand or rub his head, and he flailed when Maria picked him up to try to comfort him. My heart crumbled watching him deteriorate so severely and to see him so angry.

I dreaded each visit because it hurt too much. And I grew angrier each day that my son was enduring this torture. Ryan was in agony and his quality of life was gone, and his fighting spirit was gone along with it. He was spiraling downward on a doomed trajectory.

"Can't you see how unhappy he is? How much pain he's in?" I asked Dr. Darby. "At what point could you see ending treatment?"

"I recognize how hard this is for all of us, especially for you and Ryan," he said. "This obviously wasn't what I thought would happen. But there's still a chance for him to get through this."

"What makes you believe that?"

"Well, there is a high percentage of success in outgrowing BPD, and if we can just get Ryan through this tough period, that goal can possibly still be achieved over time."

"You've been treating him now for over a year," I said. "How can you not see that he's *not* going to outgrow it? I'm not a doctor, and I can see it clear as day." I felt sad, frustrated, and angry.

"I hear you, but ending life-sustaining treatment has to be the absolute last resort. In most cases, people choose to end life-sustaining treatment because there's no brain activity. Ryan's brain is perfectly fine."

No one other than me and the nurses could even discuss the impossible decision to end Ryan's life. How could I, as his mother, the one who loved him most of all, be the only one with enough strength and courage to face such horror? Would the doctors ever be able to see what I saw? I saw a little boy who had suffered more in his two years than most adults would suffer over a lifetime, whose face used to light up with smiles and now no longer did.

Day by day, Ryan was slipping away from us. He had stopped

fighting and was no longer the Ryan we knew. He might open his eyes from time to time, but the light was gone. Yet I was still the only one who would support removing him from the ventilator. My voice alone was not enough.

A few weeks later, Dr. Darby approached us with an option. "How would you feel about placing a DNR order on Ryan?"

"How would that work?" John asked.

"Well, if his heart stops or if he stops breathing, we will not perform resuscitation."

"I didn't know that was an option," I said.

"If he stops breathing and you don't resuscitate him, won't he die?" John asked.

"Most likely, yes."

John and I looked at each other, fear evident in our eyes. He stood and paced around the room. "I don't know. That seems extreme."

"John, Ryan isn't happy like this," I interjected. "He is in excruciating pain and is very angry. He's not getting better. Can't you see that?"

"Is that really what you think is best at this stage?" John asked Dr. Darby.

"I do," he responded.

I saw the confusion in John's eyes. "Look," I said, "This puts it in God's hands. God will determine if Ryan lives or dies. That must mean something to you." My eyes pleaded with him to agree to the DNR order.

As John conceded, I felt gratitude for Dr. Darby's ability to finally recognize Ryan's pain and recommend a path forward that took the forceful end-of-life decision out of my hands.

What a tragic decision to have to make.

Ryan's decline continued through October, this time with fevers hitting 107 and 108, but still no infection could be identified. Ryan's body was being tortured. I once again tried negotiating with God.

God, I know I'm supposed to pray for your will to be done, but this cannot possibly be what you want for my child. This cannot be your will. So I'm giving you two options. Perform a miracle and heal him, or take him. Please don't let him suffer any longer. Please.

We called on Dr. Stanton again to guide us. I desperately wanted Ryan to live, but not like this. And I couldn't bear to see him suffer any longer. My husband was only just beginning to agree.

"You must be 100 percent certain with your decision," Dr. Stanton said. "If you really want to end Ryan's treatment, you must be begging for it."

John wasn't ready to beg.

And so things continued.

One day in early November, Dr. Darby and I sat together at Ryan's bedside.

"I'm sorry," he said to me, his voice shaky. "I hope you know that I didn't want Ryan to suffer. I truly believed that he could pull through this."

"I know."

"It's now clear to me that Ryan isn't going to recover and we're only prolonging his suffering. If you and John want to stop treatment, I will support that." His eyes were filled with sorrow as he spoke.

My hand went to my mouth as tears rolled from my eyes. As much as I had thought Ryan's death was inevitable, the reality of never seeing him again shattered me.

"Oh, my God," I whispered. "Ryan is really going to die. He'll be gone forever, and I'll never get to kiss him again or touch him or love him or see him." My body convulsed with sobs. How much time would we have left together? Would he die knowing how deeply he was loved? Would he remember the smiles and the laughter, or would he only remember the last few months of pain and torture? Would there be enough time to remind him of the joy?

"We were desperate to save him, to keep him with you. I am so sorry, Susan."

I hugged Dr. Darby, my tears soaking his shoulder, realizing that he needed comfort just like I did.

John needed time to process this new reality, so I gave it to him, spending as much time by Ryan's side as I could, not knowing when it would be the last.

As the days passed, Ryan's heart began to beat erratically, "throwing PVCs" the nurses told me. Extra heartbeats were disrupting Ryan's regular heart rhythm. On the morning of November 12, I was anxious to see Ryan but had no childcare for Christian. Sensing my desperation, John said he would stay with Christian and go in to work late. I ran out the door.

When I got to the hospital, Ryan's eyes were clamped shut, groaning sounds coming from his mouth.

"How's he doing?" I asked Tara.

"Not good. His fever is still high."

He flinched when I touched his forehead. The heat from the fever penetrated my hand. "I'm here, Ryan. Mommy's here."

I sat at his bedside feeling sad and helpless. The time for playing with my son, reading to him, or massaging him was over. All I could do was sit and watch him writhe in pain.

I looked at the clock and knew I had to go home. Of the many broken, lost, sad, and empty feelings I had experienced, none permeated deeper than leaving him on that day. I didn't want to cause him pain by kissing him, so instead I whispered "I love you" in his ear. I didn't know if he could hear me.

As I entered the hospital the next day, I was surprised to see Dr. Darby standing in the lobby.

"Hi," I said, "what are you doing down here?"

"Waiting for you."

"Why?"

He hesitated. "I'm so sorry, Susan. Ryan's heart stopped."

His words hung there. For a split second, I didn't process their meaning. Then it hit me.

"He's dead? Ryan is dead? NO! NO!" I wailed. I crumbled to the lobby floor with strangled sobs.

Dr. Darby bent down beside me and held me while I wept. As people began to maneuver past the heap I'd created on the floor, Dr. Darby lifted me up. "Let's get you upstairs to Ryan."

"Is John up there?"

"He and Paula are on their way from the city."

I felt weak as my body moved down the hallway, realizing I was facing my son's death alone, as I had his birth.

"Breathe," Dr. Darby said. He had his arm around my waist as he escorted me through the door to Ryan.

My feet froze as I scanned the room. Silence. No beeping, no alarms, no motion. Ryan's eyes were closed. He appeared to be in a peaceful slumber. Our priest was at the foot of the bed, and he looked devastated. Maria and Tara were at Ryan's side, both in tears. My baby was dead. My Ryan, my firstborn, was gone, his light extinguished forever.

Maria came to me. "Do you want to hold him?" she asked.

I nodded, and she led me to the rocking chair, gently placing Ryan in my arms. The last time I'd held him had been on his birthday. Now he was gone.

He was still warm. I held his head against my chest.

"I'm sorry, RyRy, I'm so sorry." My tears rained down onto his soft brown hair. "You can rest now, sweet boy. You can finally rest." I placed kisses all over his face and head and hoped that Mary was now holding him up in Heaven giving him all the love that I no longer could.

"I will always love you, my little lamb. Never forget how much I love you." My heaving cries were not to be controlled.

John and Paula raced through the door, stopping as they came upon Ryan in my arms. I began to cry even harder. John went over to the bed and put Ryan's music into the tape player.

"Do you want to hold him?" I asked John.

"Yes." John lifted Ryan from my arms and we switched places, my heart shattering as I watched John rock his dead son.

Maria whispered something to Paula, and she started getting Ryan's things together.

Ryan's favorite song, *Somewhere Over the Rainbow*, gave us the strength to pack up the toys, books, photos, clothing, and every memory made in that hospital room and walk out the door.

Our little boy was now gone—carried off somewhere far above his beloved rainbow.

Epilogue

I stared at the tiny white casket hovering above the big black hole, desperately wanting to open the lid, grab my baby, and run. *Where would I take him?* I wondered. Home? How far would I get? Would anyone dare stop me? Could anyone stop me? Instead, I sat frozen. Afterward, I thought about going to the cemetery with a shovel and digging up the grave just so I could see him again. My thoughts weren't sane, but I didn't feel sane.

I'm not going to sugarcoat it: burying a child is hell on earth. Picking out a casket hoping it will keep him warm and dry; selecting a cemetery plot based on the proximity of trees for shade but far enough away from the railroad tracks so as not to disturb Ryan's rest; choosing a burial outfit and deciding between nice pants and a sweater so that he would look nice when he was welcomed into Heaven, or red, soft, fleece footie pajamas so that he would be comfortable. I chose the latter. I even brought a diaper to the funeral home, asking for it to be put on under the pajamas because "Ryan would need it." And, God bless the funeral director, he did as I asked.

The florist was impressed with how calm and poised I was while selecting flowers. I wasn't calm. I was numb. The beginning of my grieving process was like taking a hard punch to the gut—doubled over in pain, feeling like I couldn't breathe. But Ryan's brother, Christian, needed me. I had no choice but to stand and exhale. Thank God I had a baby to go home to.

Christian, was the sweetest and happiest of babies. He rarely cried and was a joy to care for. Never wanting to let him out of my sight, I took him everywhere with me. We became buddies. With the grief that consumed me, Christian's calm presence was exactly what my heart and my body needed. I think God knew that, and I think He blessed me with a child who would comfort and restore me at the most vulnerable and fragile point in my life. A year and a half after Christian was born, I was blessed with another child: a beautiful, healthy baby girl—my daughter, Julia. Born with a fighting spirit, Julia was energetic, persistent, and adventurous. Strength and sensitivity emanated from her big, bright, blue eyes. She challenged me on a daily basis and kept me on my toes, demanding more of me, which in turn made me demand more of myself. Julia helped me to regain my confidence. Again, God knew what I needed.

Together, Christian and Julia showed me the way forward and brought me back to life. As for the grieving process, it takes time to work through the anguish. Time doesn't *heal*, as people like to say, but it does help. Time is required in order to move through the pain and sorrow. Eventually, the waves of grief lessen in intensity and frequency. A smile is no longer forced. Laughter is no longer followed by guilt. We grow spiritually, mentally, and physically through the grief. And then we rejoice in purpose and grace.

It takes time—years, in fact—but it does happen.

As for a marriage, it's not uncommon for two parents to grieve differently, and John and I were no different. I was an Intuitive Griever: emotionally expressive, needing to talk about it. John was an Instrumental Griever: he preferred to figure it out on his own and didn't like to talk about it. He didn't understand my need for therapy. I didn't understand his lack of understanding.

Having experienced the trauma of divorce as a child, I didn't want to subject my children to a similar outcome. I wanted to forgive John for the pain his choices had caused me and Ryan, both physically and emotionally. Sadly, I didn't know how. The pain was too deep, and neither of us had the tools to fix what was broken. I had lost respect for John, and that scared me. We'd had so much love for each other that I could never have imagined feeling differently. But as time wore on, I discovered that I was feeling anything but love. Our relationship changed. How could it not? The intimacy we once shared soured and developed into resentment. I didn't know how to stop it, and in the end, my marriage became a statistic. I knew only one thing for certain: I couldn't breathe in my marriage, and I had to breathe in order to keep going.

My sister, Paula, finally met "the one": Michael. They were connected through a friend who had been visiting Ryan and me in the hospital while Paula was with me. That friend thought Paula and Michael would be perfect for each other. After a blind date, it was determined that they were. They fell in love and got married.

Paula gave birth to their first son, Jack, in 1999, and then to their second son, Andrew, in 2002. Andrew was born with a heart defect and Down syndrome. Neither my sister nor I carry the gene. Was this a coincidence, or the universe at work? You decide. Thankfully, Andrew had no other health complications and is now a thriving, athletic, high-functioning twenty-one-year-old attending college in Colorado.

Sadly, Michael, who had been fighting melanoma for many years, passed away fifteen years after marrying Paula. Their boys were just thirteen and ten at the time. Paula, with strength and grace, has raised two amazing young men. I could not be more proud of her.

One day, twenty years after Ryan's passing, Paula asked me what I wanted for Christmas. Having been told all about her amazing communication with Michael through renowned spiritual medium Rebecca Rosen in Denver, I told her, "I want a reading." Paula gifted me with an in-person reading with Rebecca at her office in Denver. This was my first time speaking with a medium, and although I had made it two decades without a direct connection to Ryan, I was hopeful he would come through to me. I did my research and read Rebecca's book, *Awaken the Spirit Within,* opening my heart and mind to divine intervention and purpose. I sat on a sofa across from her, excited and confident that Ryan would come forward. He did not disappoint.

What follows is a brief portion of the transcript from that session.

Rebecca: "Who's Ryan?"

Me: "My son who passed."

R: "Did he drown? What happened with fluid in his lungs?"

Me: "Seriously?"

R: "Yeah."

Me (taking a deep breath): "He had a very bad lung disease."

R: "That's it. He's showing me that, and he's saying that this is the last thing he felt—the pain where the swelling is." (She moves her hand up and down her throat.) "He's saying it feels tight, and pressure here, and he's trying to say then he left his body and he was free."

Me (eyes welling with tears): "That was his trach."

R: "His soul came in to teach you guys. He took one for the team here. His soul signed up to go through that, to teach all of you deeper faith and profound lessons, and your husband didn't fully get this. You have. Or you are in the process. You're getting it. It doesn't matter how long it takes you. It can take you your whole lifetime, but as long as you move in that direction. Umm...he's very playful, umm, a happy positive ball of light, and he's showing me the song over and over and over. This song will come up, it's like a cliché, like *You Are My Sunshine*. Whatever it is, it's that song." She pauses. "Is it *Somewhere Over the Rainbow?*"

At this point I began to cry, realizing that my beautiful boy was communicating with me.

R: "There's a picture of him...this is going to sound really weird, but of his feet. Do you have a picture of his feet, unless it's like a footprint?"

Me: "It's his footprints."

R: "He's smiling about that being out in sight. Do you have it sitting out somewhere?"

Me: "Yes, I have them framed and hanging on a wall in our home."

R: "He's trying to say, 'Keep my presence alive,' like he'll come and go as he can, but if you keep inviting him or acknowledging him, it's more likely it's going to happen."

A few moments later, Rebecca said, "Ryan wants you to write."

And so I did.

I can honestly say I have never been more at peace. I know that Ryan is okay, and I feel him with me every day. He sends me signs at the most perfect times, and I smile and say hi.

While I work in interior design, I remain fiercely active and committed to using Ryan's story to help doctors and medical personnel face questions of bioethics. I have also been a fund-raising volunteer for the Melanoma Research Foundation for the past eight years.

I live now with my husband, Rob, and my rescue dogs, Shay and Finley. My son and daughter are close by in New York City. I am beyond blessed and so very grateful for all of the love in my life, for the opportunities I have been given, and for all that I have learned. Ryan inspired so many people, including my children who never knew him. We talk about him, celebrate his birthday, display his photos prominently in our home, and we love him. Ryan was and still is an incredible gift, and he remains one of the strongest forces in my life.

Acknowledgments

I would not have been able to complete this book without the love and support of so many extraordinary human beings.

To Ryan, my firstborn, my angel, my inspiration, my daily reminder of all that is good in the world. Thank you for choosing me to be your mom. And to Christian and Julia. Thank you for being the lights of my life and for filling my heart. I am honored to be your mom and so proud of the magnificent adults you have become. I love you all endlessly.

To my husband, Rob, for showing me, through blinding tears, the impact of Ryan's story. Thank you for dropping whatever you were doing to read a paragraph, a page, or even a chapter. I promise to keep tissues handy in the future.

To my sister, Paula, who was like Ryan's second mom. He loved you deeply. Thank you for stepping in to be with and protect Ryan when I couldn't, for standing alongside me, and for your impassioned eulogy honoring our little angel (which I still have in Ryan's special box).

To the numerous nurses, doctors, respiratory therapists, and medical personnel who cared for and cherished Ryan during his last year. You gave me more time to love and to be loved by my exceptional little boy. You were our angels before Ryan became one. Your kindness, compassion, and support will never be forgotten. A special shout-out to Moey, Tricia, Geri, Kate, Robyn, Patty, Ida, Julio, Rikki, Alan, Jacob, Kerry, and Stuart—thank you for loving my child.

To the many friends who got me through the saddest time in my life. Thank you, Peggy, Maggie, Sherry, Margaret, Lynn, Kim, and Janet for holding me up when I wanted to crumble into a pile of rubble.

To Rebecca Rosen, spiritual medium and best-selling author. Thank you for connecting me with Ryan. You changed my life. To my publisher, Vince Font and Glass Spider Publishing. Thank you for turning my pages into my first book. From our first conversation, I knew you cared, and I knew that I and my book would be in great hands. You took a long-awaited dream and made it a reality.

And, finally, my deepest thanks to Fawn Germer, best-selling author, Pulitzer Prize nominee, keynote speaker, overall badass, and editor extraordinaire! Thank you for taking a phone call from a stranger, for listening to my story, for believing in me, and for pushing me when I was ready to give up. I couldn't have done this without you!